Mental Habits for Believers

28 Days to New Thought Patterns

Kyle Hunter

Mental Habits for Believers: 28 Days to New Thought Patterns

Copyright 2021 by Kyle Hunter. All rights reserved. Published in the United States by Monceau Publishing.

   P. O. Box 30981

   Raleigh, NC 27622

   www.Kyle-Hunter.com

No portion of this book may be copied, retransmitted, reposted, duplicated or otherwise used without the express written approval of the author. Any unauthorized use of any part of this material without permission by the author is prohibited and against the law.

Monceau Publishing or the author assumes no liability or responsibility for damage or injury to you, other persons or property arising from any use of any product, information, idea, or instruction contained in the content or services provided to you through this book. Reliance upon information contained in this material is solely at the reader's own risk.

No single book of personal or psychological advice can be used as a substitute for professional, personalized counseling or therapy if and when it is needed. Readers are encouraged to seek out professional psychological services from qualified professionals, including licensed counselors, psychologists, psychiatrists, and other qualified individuals as needed.

Quote from Dr. Nathaniel Brandon used by permission from Bantam/Random House Publishers.

Scripture quotations are taken from the *Holy Bible,* New Living Translation, copyright ©1996, 2004, 2007, 2013, 2015 by Tyndale House Foundation unless otherwise noted. Used by permission of Tyndale House Publishers, Inc., Carol Stream, Illinois 60188. All rights reserved.

ISBN 978-0-9906246-2-2

Mental Habits for Believers: 28 Days to New Thought Patterns

Mental Habits for Believers: 28 Days to New Thought Patterns

Introduction

The principles in this book can change your life. I became convinced of this several years ago during a deep personal trial. Scripture was my anchor, but I also read other books, both Christian and secular, to find ways of managing my painful thoughts and emotions. As I read, I began to see common themes which were actually tools that could enhance the way I looked at my problems and my life. These tools continue to benefit me, even though the crisis has passed.

I originally gathered these principles into a faith-neutral book, hoping it would be valuable to people from any faith background. However, as a follower of Jesus, I understood that for Christian readers, these encouraging, and life-changing ideas should be presented from another perspective. After all, the framework undergirding our lives is worlds apart from that of people without faith in Christ. The Christian believer has *special assistance* . . . access to the Almighty Father as well as His Holy Spirit and His promises. That's an enormous advantage in transforming our thoughts and habits into a way that fits with God's truth *and* our authentic selves.

I wrote *Mental Habits for Believers* to encourage Christians toward developing good mental habits within a Christian framework, acknowledging and utilizing the special help God offers us. This new edition comes a few years later, so my hope is that my additional years of understanding God's truth will spill over, making these principles even more helpful. These habits are powerful tools capable of aligning thoughts in the right direction.

In a quick survey of Christian nonfiction titles from a major distributor of Christian books, roughly half of the books help readers with some aspect of their lives. Topics included managing thoughts, changing habits, managing anger, and pursuing goals. Maybe you've read some of them and had disappointing results. These themes and more are discussed in this book but are presented in the context of developing better mental *habits* within the framework of God's relationship and commitment to us.

Because of God's grace in the world, people benefit from truths He has put into place, whether they follow Him or not. For example, telling the truth is a good principle and benefits the person doing it through good outcomes and a good reputation. People usually know it's the right thing to do. The Christian has additional reasons to be truthful. He doesn't want to grieve God, doesn't desire to sin, wants to have a good testimony before others, wants to have unbroken fellowship with God, and wants to follow Christ. All these other reasons are based on his or her *relationship* to God. This relationship gives holy energy and motivation to our ability to acquire new habits.

As you read and study *Mental Habits for Believers*, remember that you have a relationship with a heavenly Father who cares about you. This contrasts with religious principles or rituals that get filed away in our minds. Our relationship with God enables the following helpful principles to become divinely powerful ones in our lives since God is always interacting with us *and* empowering us. You'll find that the habits you are about to discover *coordinate* and *activate* God's truth in our lives.

Another way to make new mental habits a lifestyle is to study this book in a group. You'll find group discussion questions for each habit toward the end of the book.

I hope that this journey will help you know yourself better, especially in your mental habits. Some of your habits (many of which are unconscious) may have blocked you from having a fulfilling life and healthy relationships. Some may have even created sinful patterns that cast shadows over your daily relationship with God and your desire to live an effective Christian life. There are many reasons to improve mental habits. Just know that they are every bit as important as the other good habits you cultivate each day. And even more so, since they guide everything you do and feel.

Some assumptions that undergird this book

1. God loves us and desires our happiness. *John 10:10* God is for us. Have no doubt about that. He wants you to have the best, happiest and most on-target life you are meant to have.

2. God created all humans with value, whether they believe in Him or not, because He made them, and they are in His likeness. That means we have value even before we come to know Him because He made us. *Genesis 1:27*

3. Working on our lives is a good and healthy way for us to "tend the garden" that God has given us. It isn't selfish. We all acquire bad habits in our lives. It's inevitable in this fallen world. That includes our habits of *thinking*. Do you believe God wants you to improve them, with His help? He *does* want it and will rejoice in your progress! Changing mental habits is a way we bring our thoughts into alignment with what is "true, honorable and right." *Philippians 4:8*

Each chapter has reflection questions to help you to apply what you've read. I encourage you to answer them right in the book (for the paperback) or buy a notebook, if you want more space or are using an eBook or audiobook. Write your answers as well as any other reflections that the reading and Scriptures trigger for you. If you create a method for recalling and applying throughout the day what you've learned, this will lead to more lasting change.

I have no doubt that if you reflect on these principles and make them into regular habits, they can help you change your life and assure you a better future.

Kyle Hunter

Table of Contents

Introduction   5
Day One: Do I Have Mental Habits?   11
Day Two: Your Essential Mental Habit   17
Day Three: Can You Change Your Brain?   21

The 8 Mental Habits   26

Habit One: Positive Thinking
Day Four: The Power of the Positive   27
Day Five: Let's Get Positively Practical   36
Day Six: Intentional Positivity   45

Habit Two: Interpretations and Mind Frames   52
Day Seven: Interpretations and Their Impact on Us   53
Day Eight: Adjusting Interpretations   58
Day Nine: Making Mind Frames Work for You   66

Habit Three: The Habit of Self-Esteem   72
Day Ten: The Vital Importance of Self-Esteem   73
Day Eleven: A Self-Esteem Assessment   78
Day Twelve: Transforming Self-Esteem   85
Day Thirteen: Continuing the Self-Esteem Journey   93

Habit Four: Living in the Present   97
Day Fourteen: Definition and Distractions   98
Day Fifteen: The Intrusion of the Past   102
Day Sixteen: Worry and the Future Trap   106

Habit Five: Specific Thinking   115
Day Seventeen: Specific vs Global Thinking   116
Day Eighteen: Critical or Emotional Thinking?   122

Mental Habits for Believers: 28 Days to New Thought Patterns

Habit Six: The Habit of Self-Responsibility	129
Day Nineteen: Agents or Victims?	130
Day Twenty: More Powerful Than You Think	135
Day Twenty-One: Make Your Life Better	139
Day Twenty-Two: Decide to Decide (Trust is a Choice)	143
Habit Seven: The Habit of Openness	148
Day Twenty-Three: Open vs Closed	149
Day Twenty-Four: Be Curious. Be a Bridge	155
Day Twenty-Five: A Big World	161
Habit Eight: Knowing Yourself	165
Day Twenty-Six: The Rudder of Your Life	166
Day Twenty-Seven: Have You Lost Your Way?	171
Day Twenty-Eight: Glad to Meet Me	174
Putting It All Together	184
Questions for Group Discussion	191
About the Author	215

Day One

Do I Have Mental Habits?

You have probably heard that the mind is a battlefield. Maybe you have lots of first-hand experience with this truth. It isn't hard to believe, given the negative influences all around us daily. How effortless it is for us to develop unhealthy mental habits, ones that are counterproductive to our deepest desires for our lives. These negative mental habits hovers in the background even as we do our best to follow the Bible. They end up hindering or even sabotaging our attempts to live a faithful Christian life.

The book you are reading contains a collection of mental habits that form the basis of mental health. Both Christian and secular psychologists as well as many pastors agree on their importance in leading people to satisfying lives and relationships.

Here is a startling fact we might not realize: *How we think controls how we live.* Our thoughts and mental habits are a command center for our entire lives, not just the daily bits, but the long trajectories into the future. Developing healthy mental habits is essential for mentally healthy lives, contentment, good relationships, and good futures. "Guard your heart above all else for it determines the course of your life." Proverbs 4:23

It is important to emphasize that mental habits are *tools* to help us with our thought processes, but they in no way replace God's Word or His leading in our lives. If we stay in open communication with Him and attempt to follow His truth the best we can, mental habits will help us do that. Good mental habits work to promote our primary love relationship with our Creator.

Have you ever thought about *how* you think? Not necessarily how you solve problems or learn, but how your thoughts flow when you aren't paying attention? We all have mental habits, ways of thinking that are as much a routine as how we get ready in the morning or which way we go to work. Even if we have been Christians for years, we may have deeply rooted mental habits that undermine us and block the flow of joy God has for us. We may have integrated these habits into our lives over decades or years, without even knowing it. They may come from our families, giving us predispositions to certain beliefs; they may have grown out of difficult situations, leading us to believe that most people are dishonest and will hurt us.

I am choosing to call them habits, not beliefs, and here's why. Have you ever noticed how a belief guides your actions and even your feelings? These actions and feelings recur many times daily and over months and years, leading to a habit. That's called a *mental habit*. Like other habits, you repeat it regularly. And like a habit, it is often unconscious. But it *can* be changed.

Why would you want to change a mental habit? *Because what you think about determines your life experience.* Do you want the best life possible? God surely wants that for you. Your mental habits direct the course of your life according to your unique gifts and desires. And they can help you live according to God's truth.

It might be easy for you to recognize negative mental habits in other people, especially those who annoy you! Maybe you even recognize some negative habits in yourself, or lies you believe without knowing it. That's much harder because we all have blind spots. Pride or even low self-esteem block us from an honest view of ourselves.

The idea that we all have negative mental habits isn't a criticism, whether of you or others. It's simply a fact we can't escape. Usually, we aren't aware of our habits and how they might be making us unhappier or less successful than we ought to be or affecting people we care about in a negative way. A shift in these habits can transform our lives and relationships.

Mental habits can be positive or negative, productive or destructive. An example of a positive mental habit is to frequently consider yourself better off than many people in the world and to feel thankful. Studies have even shown that thankful people are generally happier people. Being thankful on a regular basis leads to good feelings and positive attitudes toward other people and about your life in general. It also helps you feel closer to God and more able to trust Him as you consider what He's done for you or has given you.

Positive mental habits lead to a greater sense of well-being and peace. They can even help you make friends, find love, get the job you want, overcome weaknesses, and accomplish your life dreams. Though many teachers and organizations promote these habits, you'll soon see that they are Biblical. Researchers, motivational coaches, pastors, and psychologists have identified the benefits of positive mental habits. What and how you think *can* change your life, your emotions, and your future.

We are all imprinted with negative influences, whether they come from family, media, friends, or our work environment. These lead us to unhelpful mental habits, hardened ruts in our mental infrastructure. Whoever you are and whatever your situation, you can improve your daily thought habits, and this will improve your life. Your habits are not a pre-ordained sentence. Positive mental habits can be learned, and unhelpful ones can be deleted. We can change our mental habits just like we can change other habits.

No one said it is easy, however. It takes time and persistence. In fact, it might be harder to change a mental habit than to change a physical one. It may be more challenging to stop worrying than to stop eating pastry every morning for breakfast. Some mental habits are more damaging to your health, both mental and physical, than an excessive pastry habit. Changing your breakfast menu will require a specific set of disciplined behaviors. Changing mental habits will require *mental* discipline.

Along with mental discipline, as mentioned in the Introduction, you'll need to exercise self-awareness. Self-awareness is vital to growth and advancement in all areas of your life, spiritual, relational, emotional, professional—*all* areas. Self-awareness will help you identify, over time, bad habits and even lies you've believed for years, bringing the unconscious to the conscious level so you can change them.

This might sound difficult, but as believers we have first-class assistance. The power of the Holy Spirit resides in us, and He will turbo-charge our efforts to do something good for ourselves that's aligned with His will. (Romans 8:26, Philippians 4:13.) If you are looking for a life coach, you can't do better!

Helping you develop positive mental habits is the purpose of this book. Maybe you aren't sure if you have unhelpful mental habits. You might not consider them necessarily harmful, but you know you could be happier and have more peace if you got rid of a pesky mental habit, such as worry or low self-esteem.

The first step is to identify some of your habits. Are they positive, neutral or counterproductive? We will look at eight more positive mental habits in all (after your Essential Habit), focusing on each one for between two and four days. This will give you time to reflect on each one and consider ways to change them. Over the course of the next 28 days, you'll see your thought patterns go from unconscious to conscious to improved.

All these habits form a roadmap that leads you toward greater joy in your life. You'll feel better and accomplish more of your objectives. Everyone wants that, right? And God wants that for you too. But you'll have to do the hard work of thinking and being honest with yourself.

As mentioned, each chapter includes reflection questions, exercises, and relevant Scriptures. The chapters aren't too long to read, but you'll want to allow enough time to reflect on what you're reading as well as work through the thought questions. You can take this book with you on the bus or subway or read it during your lunch hour. You can read it on your phone, tablet, or computer. You might not have enough time, money, or motivation to work through a 300-page book written by a famous psychologist, but you DO have time for this, a little at a time, especially if it's important to you to improve your mental habits. (By the way, the principles in this book are echoed by most well-known psychologists and self-help teachers.) If you're still not sure, just try one chapter and do the exercises. See if you don't feel better already!

You'll learn a lot about yourself as you work through each day's reading. Buy a spiral or other type notebook. Keep a journal of your observations, things you want to go back to, or questions you have for yourself. Jot down any thoughts or questions triggered by what you read. This is your private workbook, an *investment* in your growth and contentment. Its benefits are longer-lasting and less expensive than a day at the spa!

The following list contains some important skills you must bring with you on this journey, skills you already have or are willing to develop:

1. <u>Self-honesty</u>. Many people aren't used to the idea of emotional or personality *growth*. Don't let that idea intimidate you. All it means is to improve some area of your life so that you can live an even *better* life. Honesty with yourself in your private thoughts is an absolute requirement because you can't change a negative mental habit if you won't admit it is there. The more honest you are with yourself, the more you will grow personally and benefit from this book.

2. <u>Awareness of your feelings and mental state</u>. This is a hard one for some people, who aren't used to tuning into their emotions, unless they blow up in anger or fall in love. Once you develop this awareness, you'll be able to catch yourself with a negative habit (or a negative emotion triggered by a particular bad mental habit) and know what to do. Each chapter contains suggestions on changing unhelpful habits. Ask God to help you

become more aware of your feelings, thoughts, and habits before you start each day.

3. <u>Persistence</u>. Your mental habits have developed over a long time. Like other habits, these won't change in a day or two. That said, you'll likely see improvement in a short time. Persevere for long enough to go from deliberate, consistent effort (which will be necessary) to a nearly automatic habit. Many experts say it takes 21 days to form a new habit. If you focus on one habit for 3 weeks then move onto the next one, you can develop new mental habits in all these areas within 6 months. You may wish to focus on just certain ones, where you know you have a weakness or where other people may have pointed out to you that you need improvement.

If you're in a dark phase of life, it might seem more challenging to make these good habits stick, but it's even more vital, so don't give up. Undergird your efforts with prayer and keep moving ahead, despite and through the pain. Decide that you *will* develop healthy mental habits. They won't necessarily remove the discomfort of your current circumstances, but they will absolutely help you get through them with more grace and optimism. Then later, as things calm down, you'll have an arsenal of helpful habits for whatever season of life you are in.

Changing some or all these mental habits will enhance your quality of life for your *entire future* if you are willing to make a time investment now.

So, let the journey begin!

Day Two

Your Essential Habit

Before we start looking at the eight mental habits over the coming month, we'll start with the Essential Habit, which will form a protective foundation and shelter—a bunker of sorts—for the other eight habits. The Essential Habit should begin each day, before pressures and negative habits crowd in.

First, a personal story that illustrates this important habit. I spent many years in France in a ministry role. For several years, I lived there as a single woman. Later, I met and married my husband, a Christian who said he desired to do ministry there with me.

Fast forward fifteen years. My husband informed me that he no longer wanted to work in ministry nor live the Christian life. I was devastated. So began a desert period in my faith, a chapter which lasted several years. I still believed in Christ and tried to live a Christian life, still attended church, but I felt abandoned by God. My husband and I resigned from ministry and returned to the United States. Several months later, he informed me he was leaving to return to France. Our sixteen-year marriage was ending.

I was starting over in almost every possible way. I had to find a career in mid-life after more than two decades in ministry. I was back in my home country, but in a new city. And I was newly single. How to face the next phase of my life? I wasn't sure since I was still struggling in my spiritual desert.

During my final, painful year in France, I happened across a Bible verse in a cookbook. "Acknowledge and take to heart this day that the Lord is God in heaven above and on the earth below. There is no other." It was from Deuteronomy 4:39 (New International

Version.) That verse took root in the bruised places of my heart. I wasn't alone and off course. God was still on His throne, and I was still in His hand.

> Acknowledge (*stop, pay attention, realize*) and take to heart (*let it comfort you despite the turbulence, broken promises, emotional pain*) this day (*one day at a time*). The Lord is (*still*) God in heaven above and on the earth below. (*Is there anything this doesn't cover?*) There is no other.

The God who is *my* God is the ONLY God there is, and He is good. He is able to lead me one step, one day at a time.

Almost every day, I recited that verse early in the morning. I committed every part of my life and my day to God's direction, regardless of how I was feeling. It's amazing how much our weakness draws us to Him if we let it. Acknowledging our weakness to Him and reminding ourselves of His strength is in itself a healing act. It does more, too. It resets our thoughts to where they should be . . . acknowledging who He is and who we are. He is God. We are not, but we are beloved creations, His sons and daughters. He has adopted us, and we can trust Him, even when nothing else makes sense.

In subsequent weeks, months, and years, I found my way. Not by myself, but I relied on God daily to show me each faltering step. I also practiced the mental habits you're about to learn over the next 28 days. *Acknowledging Him as Father and Lord was and is my first and most essential habit of the day, taking to heart His love, leading and wisdom in my life.*

This habit will launch each day on the right footing, but you can certainly return to it throughout the day (as you will surely need to do many times. If you're human, that is.) The challenge is in making it a habit. But like all the other habits in this book, we'll work on it together and build gradually. All worthwhile changes require attention and time. This one is no exception. It will change your life and provide a firm foundation for the subsequent habits.

An important mindset principle to hold close in your heart involves the *change* that happened in your life when you came to Christ. The verse from Deuteronomy you just read was addressed to the newly freed Israelites. They had a special status as God's set-apart people, with special requirements and many exclusive blessings. As redeemed believers in Christ, we have infinitely more, as the following truths show. He has offered us the *new* covenant, which we see traced like a thread all the way through the Bible.

Here is a mere sampling of these truths, which *belong* to you, though it's your job to stand on them, remember them, believe, and appropriate them. Otherwise, they won't do you any good. Let them take you frequently back to your true identity in Christ throughout the day or week, and certainly in times of struggle, temptation, or discouragement.

"He has rescued us from the kingdom of darkness and transferred us into the Kingdom of his dear Son, who purchased our freedom and forgave our sins." Colossians 1:13-14

"By his divine power, God has given us everything we need for living a godly life. We have received all of this by coming to know him, the one who called us to himself by means of his marvelous glory and excellence. And because of his glory and excellence, he has given us great and precious promises. These are the promises that enable you to share his divine nature and escape the world's corruption caused by human desires." 2 Peter 1:3-4

The Psalmists give us many encouraging pep-talks when it comes to our daily lives. They often provide a needed thought adjustment.

One thing the Deuteronomy passage brings to my mind is the majesty and power of God. I'm reminded who He really is, His role in eternity and in the universe, though He created both. Modern day Christians tend to be casual about God, and many times the emphasis in our churches, devotional readings and songs are centered on us, not God. This is very different from the attitudes we see in the Old Testament, where much attention was fixed on God's *holiness*. Read the Exodus passage (Chapter 24) which describes Moses ascending the mountain to meet with God. The Israelites couldn't even approach the mountain but saw the clouds and fire of God's presence. In Isaiah 6 we see a similar sacred setting and humble attitude on Isaiah's part.

God has removed the barrier that existed before we believed in Christ, and He liberally expresses his love and desire to be present with us, help us, and guide us. Although these things are true, our loss of awe sometimes erodes our faith. We may have trouble expressing true worship as God deserves. We see the morning news and we can't imagine God is up to handling the crises in the world. Believe me, He is. He is not small nor powerless. And meditating on His sovereignty, His character, His power, and His faithfulness to execute his plans throughout history will help us trust Him for whatever is happening in the world and whatever we're facing today.

The Mind-Faith Connection

Real faith begins in our minds. With our minds, we choose to have faith in something we know and are convinced of, despite what we feel. That's the sign of true faith. As we do this, we often experience feelings of conviction afterward. Of course, we first must plant truth in our hearts in order to lean on it later when we need it. God doesn't program us for obedience and trust. He wants us to choose to believe the truth and trust Him every day.

Are you willing to start *each* day with this Essential Habit of humility, love, and trust? Why not exercise this habit right now, before you begin your study of the Mental Habits? Give your life now to God, acknowledge who He is as Creator *and* as your heavenly Father who cares about you, and express your trust in Him. Ask Him to guide you through this month of discovery and the creation of new, healthy mental habits.

Day Three

Can You Change Your Brain?

In Day One, you read that our thinking controls how we live. There are likely a few people who come to mind who demonstrate this (whether positively or negatively) in their daily lives. Their thinking patterns lead to either peace or emotional and relational chaos. At some level, you believe it's possible to change your thinking, or you wouldn't be reading this book! Our ability to change our thinking is great news because it means that we are not victims of circumstance. There may be times in our lives when the only thing we *can* change is our thoughts and attitudes. We influence our lives by the way we think and what we think about.

In many passages, the Bible assumes that changing our thoughts will change our lives, and for the better, if our thinking aligns with God's truth. As believers, we are more likely to drift into incorrect or destructive thought patterns than deliberately choose them. *Choosing* better patterns is harder, but essential to combat the drift into mental habits that are like deep, hard-to-change ruts.

The Best Way to Live

Throughout the Bible, we see passages that assume we have control over our thoughts (which are often interwoven with our decisions.) Here are just a few:

"Since you have been raised to new life with Christ, *set your sights* on the realities of heaven, where Christ sits in the place of honor at God's right hand. Think about the things of heaven, not the things of earth." Colossians 3:1-2. (Italics mine) We're told to set our thoughts on spiritual realities, not earthly ones, following a different framework of thinking based on our new life in Christ. We *can* do this, or God wouldn't have told us to do it.

"Don't copy the behavior and customs of this world, but let God *transform* you into a new person by changing the *way you think*." Romans 12:2 (italics mine)

"God has not given us a spirit of fear and timidity, but of power, love, and self-discipline." 2 Timothy 1:7. Some translations use the phrase "sound mind" instead of self-discipline. The spirit of a person is directed by his mind. The mind and thoughts choose what path to walk.

Can Your Brain Change?

Did you know changing mental habits can change your brain, as well? In other words, your conscious thought changes can, over time, influence the physical characteristics of your brain and even your DNA.

Dr. Caroline Leaf has done extensive work in this area. In her book, *Switch On Your Brain*, she asserts that we can actually change the physical biology of our brains through our thinking and choosing. She calls this "neuroplasticity," which has support from many scientific studies. Changing our mental habits changes the wiring of our brains. Neurogenesis is the birth of new brain cells, which occurs daily. Nothing in our minds is fixed from birth, or even in adulthood. Throughout our lives, we are able to change our thoughts and the physical makeup of our brains. In this way, in the words of Dr. Leaf, you can do your own brain surgery! The mind controls the brain, not the other way around. This is good news, since we have control over our minds.

As a scientific researcher who is also a Christian, Dr. Leaf supports her research with Biblical passages throughout her book. Not only that, but she provides ample scientific background research from multiple studies spanning decades. If you need to be convinced by the scientific community that your brain *can* change, or if you're simply intrigued by this topic, read her fascinating book.

Dr. Leaf also states that a change in thinking can also lead to a change in DNA. Why is that important? A change in DNA may reroute a negative hereditary predisposition into a positive one. So, changing your thoughts leads you a happier, more productive, and Biblical life, but also a healthier one.

Are you surprised by this? God wired your brain in such a way that it is moldable, changeable. Our past thought patterns don't need to define our futures. Not only does God give us the means to change our thoughts (and the command), but He actually *changes* our physiology as we build new patterns. This is an exciting fact that leads us to further invest in building healthy and Biblical mental habits.

Steps for the Journey

Record your reactions to what you just read. Are you surprised? Motivated? Intimidated? God will give you all the help you need to do your own "brain surgery" through His indwelling Spirit.

You'll learn several positive mental habits in this book. Are there any that come to your mind that you are already aware of or sparked by what you've read so far? Make a list of habits you know would be helpful in rewiring your thought patterns.

Are there specific Scriptures that spoke to you in this chapter?

Read the following passages and record how they speak to your heart in view of changing your mental habits.

1 Corinthians 2:8-16 (This is a longer passage, but there's a lot in it that will challenge and encourage you!)

Deuteronomy 30:19-20

Colossians 3:1-4

Philippians 4:8

1 Peter 3:15

Ephesians 1:21-23

Revelation 1:17-18

Mental Habits for Believers: 28 Days to New Thought Patterns

What do the previous passages imply about your mind, decisions and will?

The 8 Mental Habits

Habit One

The Habit of Positive Thinking

Day Four

The Power of the Positive

We've heard the mantras for positive thinking: Look on the bright side. Expect the best. Don't dwell on the problems. We might believe this means putting on a happy face, so that we appear to be rejoicing and trusting God (even if we're not.)

Does having a positive outlook about our lives mean that we ignore the realities in front of us? Some people adhere to a negative outlook, calling it "realistic" or "mature". Usually, these same people don't seem any happier (or godly) for having achieved maturity and realism.

What it is. What it isn't.

The habit of positive thinking doesn't mean ignoring bad news or being irresponsible. It is a way of life, circumstances, feelings, people, and a future that hopes and believes the best. It means choosing in advance how we'll focus our minds on whatever comes in our day. We acknowledge both negative and positive, but we *choose* to think of the positive aspect. Choosing the positive side boosts our self-esteem, enables gentler, kinder reactions to others and makes us feel more hopeful about our lives. More importantly, it also reflects our faith in God's goodness, sovereignty and undergirding of our lives.

This doesn't mean we ignore the difficult events that inevitably happen. And it doesn't mean we don't do what we can about a situation. It *does* mean we choose not to *dwell* on the negative, or passively get sucked into a negative mindset (which invariably leads to negative emotions). It involves an active decision, a choice.

Negative thinking is such an epidemic in our culture, most people consider it as normal. Every area of society seems to thrive on the negative: movies, news, television shows, daily conversation in families, among friends, or co-workers. The truth is, both negative and positive realities exist around us every day, but we are predisposed to seeing the negative. In periods of history, this vigilance for danger helped people protect themselves and their families. Today, it's just a bad habit, one that takes a toll on our happiness, giving us a sense of dread and anxiety and a feeling that the world is not a safe place for us. It triggers our reflex to complain and look at the dark side. This is largely subconscious but over time it becomes a powerful habit that is difficult to change. Researchers in several studies have found that habitual negative thinking creates neural pathways in the brain, which makes the habit harder to break.

Even Christian believers sometimes fall into the trap of focusing on negative events or situations and complaining about them. Having faith in a loving Heavenly Father sometimes does little to steer our thoughts in a restful, positive direction. Some believers complain and worry as much or more than nonbelievers. Seems like a paradox, doesn't it?

The Hazards of Negative Thinking

This habit affects your relationships too. Remember the last time you were in the company of a complaining or negative person. You may have felt a vague sense of discomfort, a desire to get away from that person. You might have been tempted to refute the gloom or to change the subject. Or worse, maybe you were drawn into the person's discourse about what went wrong or what could go wrong. You joined in and everyone walked away feeling sadder, more pessimistic, and more hopeless. You were the victim of a bad news dump.

Better to avoid people like that. But are *you* the negative person that upbeat, happy people want to avoid? Are you the one who dumps a negative outlook on the people around you? How is your worldview any different from someone who doesn't know God?

Negativity might make you unpopular but lurking in the shadows of pessimism are deeper dangers that affect your long-term happiness and even your health. According to both medical and psychological studies, negative thinking has an adverse effect on memory, sleep, and immunity. Negative expectations hinder the process of physical healing or therapy. Healthcare professionals call this phenomenon the *nocebo* effect. Like the placebo effect with medications, the nocebo effect influences outcomes either positively or negatively merely by expectation. Chronic negative thinking changes brain chemistry, potentially affecting the heart, the endocrine system and even the rate of mortality. A pattern of negative thinking leads to chronic anxiety and depression as well. And if that isn't enough, negative thinking blinds us to seeing positive opportunities right in front of us.

Instead, try this: "Do everything without complaining and arguing, so that no one can criticize you." Phil. 2:14-15. The verse goes on to encourage each one of us to shine like bright lights. Lights of grace, encouragement, and gratitude. How much the world needs that!

A more important truth undergirds the ability to think positively and that is our worldview regarding God's control in our world. This provides a reliable framework for optimism. Do we believe He is powerful and loving? Consider the passage from Day Two in another Bible version (New Living):

"So, remember this and *keep it firmly in mind*: The Lord is God both in heaven and on earth, and there is no other." (Italics mine) Deuteronomy 4:39. Every day.

Underlying Beliefs

A person's underlying beliefs about life will make it either easier or harder to apply these principles of positive thinking. Someone who has had several unfortunate events in her life, or a difficult background, may develop harmful beliefs, whether known or subconscious. She may firmly hold to convictions such as:

People are cruel

The world is unfair, especially to people like me (race, nationality, income, age, etc.)

God doesn't care about me

I'll never be loved

Where did her beliefs come from? They are her global interpretations about life in general and *her* life in particular. As long as she holds to these damaging beliefs, she will struggle to develop the habit of positive thinking. She must attack her wrong beliefs at the root and redefine them. *Then* she can form a healthy foundation for positive thoughts and attitudes.

An Evil Source of Negativity

As if we didn't have enough sources of negative thoughts hitting us, whether from our past, our self-esteem or our circumstances and influences, we have yet one more. It is powerful, and it's evil. As redeemed children of God, we have an enemy, Satan, and his minions. We're told he prowls around like a lion looking for someone to devour. (1 Peter 5:8) Satan has no power over our souls, but he works against us by planting thoughts in our minds. He does this with amazing accuracy as he targets our weaknesses and vulnerabilities. How? Because he observes us. He knows our fears, our childhood wounds that surface from time to time. He can't read our minds, but he can plant thoughts.

This is a vital reason to guard your mind and change your mental habits. As you stay anchored in the Word of God, you'll be able to distinguish truth from error. This is also an important reason to know your vulnerabilities and strengthen them with truth. Paul addresses this very danger when he tells the Ephesians to "hold up the shield of faith to stop the fiery arrows of the devil." (6:16) Our shield of faith is based on God's truth. Satan's fiery arrows are attacks on the truth right there on the battlefield of our minds.

One of the enemy's favorite strategies is his oldest trick, causing us to doubt God's goodness and all we know about his character. He did this in the Garden of Eden as he caused Eve to doubt God's good motives for her life. He also caused her to doubt God's pure character, convincing her that God was holding out on her. Unfortunately, it worked, and he's never stopped using this tactic with believers.

As you get better at identifying lies you believe, many of them are against God, who is the lover of your soul, the only one who loves and accepts you unconditionally. *There is no darkness in Him.* God's way is perfect (Psalm 18:30). Satan would love to have you doubt God's good plans for you, His character, His love for you and His desire to bless you. Your enemy wants you to doubt these things, and he'll succeed if you let him. And that will weaken you in every area of your life. Be on guard for his strategies. The apostle Paul wrote to the early Church that we are *not* unaware of Satan's strategies, and that we are not fighting against flesh and blood, but against evil authorities. (Ephesians 6:12). Don't be unaware. Because anytime we're unaware of any enemy, especially one like him, we're vulnerable. Keep hiding in God's promises and his strength and, if you slip off the path of truth, use the mental habits you learn in this book to steer you back again.

I experienced this just recently. I'd prayed for years for positive results in an area of my work. One day, the thought came to me that if God didn't want me to succeed in that area, I was working for nothing, because He would block me. My emotions started to sag, then I caught myself. God is not against me. God is *for* me (Romans 8:31). If He delays the result I most want, He has a good and loving reason and perfect timing.

I started reciting Scriptures that confirm God's good plans for me, His promises for my future and the way He uses even long, difficult periods of waiting for our ultimate good and His glory. (Psalm 138:8) As I focused on that, I could almost feel the enemy slink away as my thoughts changed direction. I felt stronger because I was aligned with the truth. I knew God was for me and the answers to my prayer were entirely within his perfect will and timing. (Jer. 29:11) Truths such as, "Each day the Lord pours his unfailing love upon me, and through each night I sing his songs, praying to God who gives me life" filled my mind (Psalm 42:8).

Paul's bold statement to the church in Corinth sums it up, and is a vital reminder for us, as well: "The weapons we fight with are not the weapons of the world. On the contrary, they have divine power to demolish strongholds. We demolish arguments and every pretension that sets itself up *against the knowledge of God*, and we take captive every thought to make it obedient to Christ." 2 Corinthians 10: 4-5 NIV (italics mine) Note the strong words: demolish, fight, take captive. These are war words. You are in a war for your mind, but God has equipped you to fight back.

The Benefits of Positive Thinking

Just as we've seen that negative thinking is linked with poor health, studies spanning more than fifty years show that positive thinkers generally have better health up into older age. On average, they add between seven and ten years to their life spans. Populations around the world with long life spans are also found to be optimistic. Learning the habits of positive thinking will strengthen your body's defense against disease and impact your emotional well-being. This should come as no surprise since health and mental health professionals increasingly recognize the link between the mind and the body.

The good news is that with some focused effort and a clear choice on your part, you can change this habit, gradually transforming your negative neural pathways into positive ones. The more you think positively, the more you *will* think positively, since it feeds on itself. Then the more you are positive, the happier you will feel, the more empowered and the more hopeful for the future.

It is a powerful habit that unlocks benefits for your self-esteem and well-being. Over time you'll see potential opportunities instead of problems. You'll feel empowered instead of passively impotent. You'll discover an increased ability to accomplish your personal goals and dreams. You'll experience a deeper connection to God's truth and His loving hand on your life. On top of all that, you'll *feel* better, happier. It's worth it for your future contentment to learn this valuable habit.

Steps for the Journey

Do you tend to think and speak positively or negatively? If you're not sure, notice how you speak to others and what thoughts frequently come to your mind. Write down your observations.

What points in today's reading stood out to you?

Have there been any undesirable results from negativity in your life?

How might change your life to become more positive? (You'll find practical suggestions in this section and the readings for the next two days.)

Are there specific areas in your thoughts that you could identify as spiritual lies embedded in your heart by your enemy, Satan? What are they?

What verses from God's Word contradict these lies?

Take a moment now to renounce the lies and affirm God's truth over them. Do this regularly, to remind your subconscious lies that their days are numbered.

Write a list of at least 8 things that are going RIGHT in your life, things you're thankful for. Reread this list **each day** as you begin the day or before you leave home. Keep a copy in your phone or on an index card to carry with you or post in your house. Refer to it during the day. Add new things as you go along or update your list monthly. After you write the list, thank God for these things.

1)

2)

3)

4)

5)

6)

7)

8)

In the coming week, try to become more aware of your patterns of thoughts and speech. If you catch yourself saying something negative, jot it down in a small notebook. Include a phrase about what you were talking about and over time you'll see a pattern. The first goal is to build an *awareness* of your thought and speech patterns to see if they lean toward negative or positive. That way you'll shift them in the right direction!

"May the words of my mouth and the meditation of my heart be pleasing to you, O Lord, my rock and my redeemer." Psalm 19:14

Day Five

Let's Get Positively Practical

Negative thinking is a *very* common habit, and most people are unaware of it. Listen to yourself as you speak with others. Listen to them as well and observe. You will gradually become more sensitive to the prevalence of negativity. The more you develop awareness, the more you'll catch yourself. Negativity will become more difficult to listen to. Awareness is the first step.

As you tune into your current habits, consider *why* you speak and think the way you do. Is it merely a habit, one that doesn't necessarily reflect your attitude about life? Is it reinforced by the people you hang around, the news or programs you listen to and watch? Or does it reflect deeper fears you may have about your life and future? If your fears and beliefs are influencing your outlook, spend some time examining them. Write out what you're afraid of on a piece of paper. If you're not sure, consider what dark thoughts come often into your mind as you go through your day, or in the middle of the night. Ask yourself if they are realistic or not. Can you do something about them? Many times, you can, and just making a plan will make you feel better. Talk about these with a friend, or if you prefer, a counselor. Turn these fears over to God, knowing He is big enough to handle them. Getting to the root of negativity will take you closer to changing the pattern.

If you're afraid of something you can do nothing about, that's another story. These worries are useless burdens for you, burdens that God can handle. As a believer, that's the only correct way you can respond. Depending on how much you typically struggle with worry, you may need to turn these things over many times per day. Beware of fear catalysts, such as certain news programs. Some people should back off almost completely from news or weather programs because the emotional toll of worry is too great. If you're not sure if that describes you, observe your emotional reaction after watching the news. And don't forget that much of it is exaggerated to increase ratings and viewers.

Does negativity enter your speech? Beware of phrases like "It's a shame that . . .", "I sure wish . . .", or "Wouldn't you know that . . .". These phrases lead your focus toward whatever is going wrong (or might) in your life. As we verbalize our negative thoughts, they have a greater hold on us. Not only that, but they also sprinkle a dose of sadness and pessimism on the people around us.

What is the *source* of your negative thoughts? Is it reliable? Is the information even true? Maybe you're worried about possible criminal activity in your town or upset about proposed laws. Can you find out facts about this? Maybe there's nothing to be concerned about. Or put your fear into words and ask yourself, if this happens, how will I respond? Sometimes it helps to ask, "What is the worst thing that is likely to happen?" then "How will I cope, and what will I do? Is this something God can't handle?" This will put the fears into perspective.

Maybe your negative thoughts have to do with worries about the future or regrets about past events. We will look at these in more depth in a later chapter.

Positive Thinking in Action

Let's meet Laura to see a practical response in daily life. Laura drags herself out of bed to go to work on a Monday morning, like every other day. She feels lethargic and dreads the week ahead. She hates her job, which she has held for the last two years. She pictures people there she doesn't like, including her boss, who makes her feel stupid.

She walks into the bathroom to prepare and sees the card she taped on her bathroom mirror bearing the words: "What's good about this situation?" She mulls this over. What's good? At first, it's difficult for her to come up with anything. She forces herself to find something good, and with effort, she does. She has a job and isn't unemployed. She is healthy enough to get up and go to the office. She has skills that make her employable. She trusts that God has a new place of employment for her and will give it to her in His timing.

Laura glances out the window and adds to her list: it's a lovely spring day, and the pear blossoms are just coming out on the trees. How beautiful! She decides to walk to a further bus stop so she'll enjoy the morning. What else? Oh yes, one more important thing. She isn't trapped. She *can* change jobs and plans to do so. She has already started looking at openings, and every day that she stays at her current job until she finds a better one gives her that much more experience.

How do you think Laura feels by this time? A lot better. Empowered and hopeful. She feels thankful and ready to enjoy the spring morning. She makes a picnic to take outside during her lunch break and plans to look at job postings during her coffee break. She prays for these concerns and steps, but her positive outlook also propels her to proactivity and positive feelings, as well as the ability to look beyond her current circumstance. She remembers God's presence and strength, and she gets busy on *her* part.

Trials, Big and Small

Everyone has trials. Some are small, irritating ones, kind of like gnats buzzing around your face. They're annoying, but they're temporary. Spam phone calls. Tech problems. You know the kind. Sometimes they come in multiples and it's easier to get negative because they don't seem to ever stop. It's easy to let those things grow in importance in our minds and open the door to negativity.

Then there are the big ones. The kind that seemingly go on forever. An illness, a job search, a difficult relationship. Yes, these are hard, and it's even harder to stay positive when you don't see an end in sight. You need special help. You need a community around you, positive input, and a continual reminder that God is good and hasn't forgotten you. Start your day in God's Word, seeing it not as a duty, but as a means of equipping your heart for the day. No soldier goes into battle without preparation and proper equipment. You'll need to cling tightly to God's promises and therein is your strength against enemy thoughts as well as lousy circumstances.

Put verses on your mirror or wall, dashboard or desk and meditate on them. Savor them like a luscious dessert (or clutch at them like a life preserver) until they sink into your heart and carve a hole in your doubts. Do whatever it takes to remember that He is *for* you. You won't stay locked in negativity for very long!

Consider, too, that the original recipients of these verses were undergoing intense persecution, ostracism for their faith and martyrdom. God's words to us are the same as to those early Christians. They comfort us in all our trials, big and small.

The next chapter will give you additional steps to help during difficult times. For right now, take time to reflect on God's perspective of our trials. He sees the big picture and knows the outcome.

"So we are always confident, even though we know that as long as we live in these bodies we are not at home with the Lord. For we live by believing and not by seeing." 2 Corinthians 5:6-7.

"Dear brothers and sisters, when troubles come your way, consider it an opportunity for great joy. For you know that when your faith is tested, your endurance has a chance to grow. So let it grow, for when your endurance is fully developed, you will be perfect and complete, needing nothing." James 1:2-4

"Can anything ever separate us from Christ's love? Does it mean he no longer loves us if we have trouble or calamity, or are persecuted, or hungry, or destitute, or in danger, or threatened with death? No, despite all these things, overwhelming victory is ours through Christ, who loved us." Romans 8:35, 37

"Through your faith, God is protecting you by his power until you receive this salvation, which is ready to be revealed on the last day for all to see. So be truly glad. There is wonderful joy ahead, even though you have to endure many trials for a little while. These trials will show that your faith is genuine. It is being tested as fire tests and purifies gold—though your faith is far more precious than mere gold. So when your faith remains strong through many trials, it will bring you much praise and glory and honor on the day when Jesus Christ is revealed to the whole world." 1 Peter 1:5-7

What are your most common negativity traps, whether big or small? Reframe these situations as growth opportunities. Pray that God will mold your character and supervise your learning process through these trials.

Steps for the Journey

How much negativity do you observe in the various places where you spend your day?

How negative is your environment on a scale from 1 to 5? (1 is the least, 5 the most.)

Have you noticed you have frequent negative thoughts or comments?

What is the most frequent subject for your negative thoughts and comments?

Is this negative focus just a bad habit or does it reflect deeper fears in your life? If you have deeper fears, what are they?

Does it help you feel less fearful when you think about and express negative things?

What could you do differently with your negative feelings and fears? In what ways can you activate your faith in God in face of your fears?

What if you knew that your current strengths and positive coping skills were the result of a previous hardship you had endured? How would you look at that hardship in the light of this knowledge?

What might God be trying to teach you through your current problems (big or small)? How can you cooperate with His purposes?

Like the example of Laura in the chapter, write the following words on a 3 x 5 card and keep it in your purse, wallet or on your mirror or dashboard: *What is good about this situation?* Look at it frequently and you'll start to build a mental habit of positive thinking. Be creative as you ask, *What's good about this*? Make as long a list as possible. Keep in mind God's promises to make all things work together for good (even if they aren't in themselves good) for those who love Him. (Romans 8:28.)

Pay attention to what influences get into your heart and head. Guard the doorways to your mind. Be careful who you spend time with and the effect they have on you. If you spend time around negative people, try to limit your contact with them. If you can't do this, counter their negative comments with a positive one, or just change the subject. (Don't be surprised if this irritates them.)

Be conscious of what you listen to or watch that might funnel negative messages into your mind. I know a woman who won't go to movies because so many of them disturb her. This may seem extreme and unnecessary to most people, but in her case, she knows she's vulnerable. What are your vulnerabilities? Horror movies or movies in general? News? Political programs? Editorials? Conversations at the water cooler or over lunch?

I should limit my time with . . .

I am especially vulnerable to negative thinking when I (activity) . . .

Sometimes our negative thoughts center on a person (or whole groups of people) who has hurt us or who we dislike. (Yes, even Christians sometimes do this.) We may mentally stew about that person or talk about him or her, assuming evil or selfish motivations. Stop it. Right now. Most of the time you don't know what the person's motivations are, and assuming the worst will stir up your insides with anger and frustration.

As you speak about that person to someone else, you risk stirring up others as well, starting rumors and being seen as spiteful or judgmental. You probably don't want that reputation. *Assume the best about people.* There could be several reasons for the behavior that is bothering you. The short-tempered cashier probably has personal problems that have nothing to do with you. Angry people are often simply hurting people. Try compassion. Believe the best. (1 Corinthians 13:7)

If there has been a conflict or a wrong done, do your best to resolve it by talking it out (not accusing, but by asking questions and talking), especially if it's a close relationship. If this isn't possible, decide that you will let it go. Try to catch yourself whenever you stew over that person.

I am often frustrated with . . .   because of . . .

Two different possible explanations for his/her behavior/comment/action are:

    1)

    2)

Let love and faith win.

Read the following verses and summarize how they help you think more positively.

    2 Corinthians 4:7-10

Philippians 2:14-16

Colossians 1:11

Philippians 3:20

"The Lord is my light and my salvation---so why should I be afraid?" Psalm 27:1

"And we know that God causes everything to work together for the good of those who love God and are called according to his purpose for them." Romans 8:28

Day Six

Intentional Positivity

When you have a negative thought, immediately counter it with a positive one. This habit will take time to develop, but soon it will be second nature. For example, you get annoyed because you went to a restaurant and had poor service. When negative thoughts begin brewing about that situation, say to yourself, "They must be having an off day today," or something else that springs from compassion. Cut off the negative thought before it develops. And consider what God would have you learn through that situation. Maybe He wants to strengthen your patience, wants you to show kindness and compassion to someone, or give you an opportunity to make a good choice with your focus.

Try a reframing exercise: Take a piece of paper or a computer document and write out all your complaints about your life. Don't skip anything. Your insensitive roommate, your lousy job, health problems, and so on. When you are finished go back and after *each phrase* write in parentheses a *reframing* of that negative situation. In other words, put the same sentence in a more positive light. So, next to your phrase "My car broke down and I have to take the bus to work for the next two weeks," you'll write "I get to catch up on reading or meet interesting people during my bus ride to work."

Or "No one invited me for Thanksgiving dinner this year," is followed by, "Since I don't have plans for Thanksgiving, I can invite some friends over or rent a condo at the beach." Highlight these reframes in red or yellow and read only the colored sentences. You could also find inspiring quotes or Bible verses and tape them to the fridge, a mirror, or your desk to help you redirect your thoughts. Your gratitude-meter will bump up a few notches as you redirect your focus.

Of course, you shouldn't reframe into a positive light a really bad situation that you have the power to change. Don't accept a terrible predicament, such as an abusive job or spouse, or piles of debt, for example, and try to see it in a positive light. Do everything you can to change your situation whenever it is appropriate.

The Thinking-Feeling Cycle

Are there certain negative thoughts that pop up frequently? What kinds of emotions normally follow? What does that say about your beliefs, or your feelings about that aspect of your life? It's helpful to keep a daily thought/emotion journal. Note how your thoughts affect your moods. What kinds of events trigger negative thoughts?

Uncomfortable emotions are often an early warning sign that a negative thought pattern is underway. You feel tightness in your stomach or tension in your shoulders. Other times you'll notice the thought first, then the negative emotions come trotting faithfully alongside. Tracking emotions and thoughts (and linking them) helps you better understand the cause of the negative emotion as well as the underlying belief. This helps you to choose your response, thereby changing the pattern. You might also identify something in your life that you need to change.

When you spot a gathering of negative thoughts, try to empty your mind. Imagine a pail with water leaking out or a popped balloon. Release your negative thoughts, but quickly replace them with positive ones, for example, God's promises. Remember His sovereignty and character. It's not all up to you! Relax your whole body as you think of Him. Imagine placing these thoughts into God's hands.

Writing down the positive reframes will help too, as will speaking or repeating them aloud. Picture your favorite place, or someplace you want to be or visit. A Caribbean beach, a flowering valley or your own back yard. Have a Scripture verse handy that speaks to your particular struggle. Reread this often.

Challenge the validity of your negative thoughts. They are likely distortions of reality. Replace them with more positive ones. Look at the big picture, not just at the one detail that isn't going well.

Jinxing Ourselves

Are you sometimes afraid of success? Are you afraid of what will happen next? This may be a reason why positive thinking hasn't worked for you yet. We often punish ourselves for our failures. We believe we deserve to be punished so we sabotage ourselves. This isn't always conscious. What are the consequences of success? Are there any uncomfortable results you might be subconsciously trying to prevent?

We may have negative expectations. If they do happen, we say, "I knew it. This always happens to me." This only reinforces your prediction. As an experiment, try the opposite. Expect the best. Picture it in your mind in graphic detail. Thank God in advance that He will cause all things to work together for good, as He promised. You have nothing to lose!

Be patient with yourself if it takes a few days or weeks to see change. Be persistent and stay aware of subtle shifts in your emotions and outlook. And don't forget to take notes in your journal and thank God for any positive shifts that you detect in your perspective.

When Things are Really Bad

Sometimes our life circumstances hit rock bottom. You read about this reality yesterday, and hopefully, God's perspective enlarged your view and encouraged you.

When you're dealing with hard times, ask yourself if you are able to change *anything*. Be honest. We might conclude we can't change our circumstances, but we *can* change a few things. If we can't attack the source of difficulty, try for small changes that make you feel better in the short run. Sometimes your focus is all you *are* able to change, but that alone can make a huge difference.

What if your pain comes from another person? Evaluate your response and see if you can change your life in some small way so you'll be more content, despite that person's choices or predicament. Talk to him if you think this will help. Can you limit your contact with this person or even remove him from your life? If you can't, improving or appreciating other parts of your life will help you feel better.

What if there is a disastrous turn of events? Look for the best results from the situation. What can you draw out of the experience and build upon? Many times, good outcomes will accompany a bad event, if you give it time to play out. For example, maybe you lost your job, but you met a new friend in the unemployment line. Or maybe the loss of the job will push you to start the business you've dreamed about but put off. Positive secondary outcomes help us mentally offset unfortunate events, that is, if we look for and find them. Ask God to help you see the silver lining, the hidden opportunity.

Having positive expectations and a positive attitude doesn't mean things will *always* work out or have a stunning bigger meaning. At times, we won't know the answers. Ever. In these cases, we need to simply stir that bitter piece into the greater mixture of life, and then let it go. This, too, is a form of positive thinking. That acceptance will help set us free from painful regrets, so we don't miss any of our good future.

If you are going through a difficult phase of life (and even if you're not), don't forget to treat yourself kindly on a regular basis. Be good to yourself in a way that's meaningful to you. It might be a bunch of fresh flowers, seeing a movie, buying a new piece of clothing, going for a walk in your favorite part of town or with a special friend or soaking in a bubble bath.

Steps for the Journey

Is there any situation in your life that requires, not positive thinking, but change on your part? What is it, and what will you do about it?

How often does conscious positive thinking lead you to increased thankfulness?

Thankfulness will be an enormous help in becoming less negative. It's pretty difficult to be thankful and negative at the same time. If you do find yourself feeling thankful about something, go ahead and thank God at that moment or as soon as possible. Positivity and thankfulness go hand in hand, supporting one another.

Note your current patterns of thinking and a date in your journal. Summarize and date any victories and progress that you observe. Use your notebook to write your lists of positives and things you are thankful for. Read over that list daily (or more than once daily).

<u>My victories in overcoming negative thinking</u>

Date:
What happened:

How I felt:

Date:
What happened:

How I felt:

Date:
What happened:

How I felt:

You can find other tools to help you look at your life and the world in a more optimistic, hopeful, and positive way. Being more positive will be infectious. You'll probably notice people wanting to be around you more and more. You'll smile more and generally feel better about your life. Misery may love company with other negative folks, but a positive habit of thinking is what the whole world craves and needs.

"For you know that when your faith is tested, your endurance has a chance to grow. So let it grow, for when your endurance is fully developed, you will be perfect and complete, needing nothing." James 1:3-4.

"Live wisely among those who are not believers and make the most of every opportunity. Let your conversation be gracious and attractive so that you will have the right response for everyone." Colossians 4:5-6.

"And now, dear brothers and sisters, one final thing. Fix your thoughts on what is true, and honorable, and right, and pure, and lovely, and admirable. Thing about things that are excellent and worthy of praise." Philippians 4:8.

Key Thought: You can choose what you think about.

Habit Two

Interpretations and Mind Frames

Day Seven

Interpretations and Their Impact on Us

Whatever happens to us passes through a filter we all have. This filter is called *interpretations*. How we interpret events is subjective, individual, and changeable. How we view experiences or circumstances influences our feelings and subsequently, our actions and possibly even the course of our lives. Our interpretations take us way off course or bring us back. They may cause either misery or contentment. In this section we'll see how interpretations work, how they sabotage us, and how to change them so they benefit us. We'll also learn about changing our "mind frame," when we have runaway negative emotions.

Like other mental habits, this one is probably so ingrained in your subconscious, you may not realize it is there. In this chapter, you'll have a look at how you interpret what happens in your life and become aware of your patterns.

The habit of good interpretations works hand-in-glove with positive thinking. When you think positively, you choose the slant of your viewpoint *as* you approach each day, and you expect favorable outcomes. Interpretations are a positive grid through which you see events and situations that you have encountered. The event comes first, and your interpretation follows. Changing an interpretation for the better is like giving yourself a thought-adjustment. As Christians, we have a framework, Biblical faith, that makes it easier to apply the principles in this chapter.

How we interpret events and situations affects our sense of well-being. Here's how it works. We see a situation and interpret it in a certain way that may have nothing to do with reality. For example, a couple may say, "Our son isn't coming home from college for the summer." Their interpretation: "He doesn't want to be with us." If the couple believes this interpretation, naturally it will cause pain and may damage the relationship. But maybe their son, being twenty years old, wants to spend his summer doing things young people like to do. Maybe he wants to take a trip with friends his age or work near his campus and take a summer class. The real reason has nothing to do with the parents and more to do with the son's desires and goals. The situation is neutral, but the interpretation ignites it like dynamite.

What Influences Our Interpretations?

In his book *Life Strategies*, Dr. Phil McGraw states that there is no reality, only perception. What he means is that no matter what happens in your life, the way you interpret that event, or assign meaning, is up to you. He calls our interpretations "filters," often arising from our childhood or past experiences, and the assumptions, faulty or not, that come out of them. A situation may still be a regrettable or tragic one, but how we respond to it is determined by our interpretation of the event. That response makes a bad thing worse, or it helps you make the best of it or even turn it around for a positive end result. The event or reality may not be our fault. It might be the result of someone else's mistake or cruelty, or a random bad event. We didn't control any of that. Yet, we can control or at least influence our interpretation and our response.

People may cling to an unfortunate interpretation of an event because of expectations they received in their childhood. This is a common, though not the only, cause of a bias toward a negative interpretation. That tendency may also rise from a low self-esteem or a subconscious belief that we don't deserve any better. Sometimes we group similar events in our minds and produce a statement about ourselves or about our lives, such as "I'm just unlucky," or "I can't seem to ever get ahead," using those examples as proof.

A similar idea to filters is something psychologists call "explanatory style." This simply means the way you habitually explain an event or situation to yourself. Are you more likely to take the blame for a negative event that you had no direct control over? Or will you most often attribute its cause to something external?

Your filter might be related to you. You say, "I always make mistakes," or "Bad things always seem to happen to me," or "I'm not very popular." This affects how you interpret people's responses to you. (See the chapter on self-esteem for more on this.)

Or maybe everything is always someone else's fault, never yours. Your explanatory style may reinforce the idea that you're a helpless victim, and you had nothing to do with your current state. Maybe your filter causes you to stack everything against yourself, making yourself even more helpless in your own mind.

Here's another unhelpful habit we may have. Do you see a negative event as permanent or temporary? If we see a negative event as temporary, we get through it more easily with a better attitude. Do you view the negative habit, the weakness, the event as something that can't be changed? Or do you feel you have influence over it? In general, would you say you have an optimistic or a pessimistic explanatory style? An empowered or helpless one? Try to notice your patterns. They could have a huge impact on your level of stress *and* your contentment.

Steps for the Journey: Interpretations

Identify a situation or two that made you feel embarrassed, frustrated, self-conscious, etc. List your interpretation of what happened.

Situation 1:

My Interpretation:

Situation 2:

My Interpretation:

Using the same situations, write at least 3 *other* possible interpretations for each situation. For example, if your friend at work appeared angry when you came in, she doesn't necessarily dislike you. 1) She could be catching a cold and not feel well, 2) She could be distracted by her own work or problems, 3) She didn't see you, and 4) She was angry at another person or herself.

Situation 1

Possible reason #1:

Possible reason #2:

Possible reason #3:

Situation 2

Possible reason #1:

Possible reason #2:

Possible reason #3:

Do you default to negative interpretations for most situations you encounter?

Do you usually only come up with one possible explanation and it's a negative one?

How does your faith come into your interpretation of those and other events? What changes would this make?

What can you do to develop the habit of *multiple feasible interpretations*? Write your thoughts and ideas in your notebook or in the following space. Then write your specific action plan for changing your interpretations.

"Now we see things imperfectly, like puzzling reflections in a mirror, but then we will see everything with perfect clarity." I Corinthians 13:12

"Understand this, my dear brothers and sisters: you must all be quick to listen, slow to speak, and slow to get angry." James 1:19

Day Eight

Adjusting Interpretations

As we walk through our days, we talk to ourselves in our heads. We do this all day long. You may not be aware that you do this, but if you develop a habit of tuning into your daily dialogue, this will help you with all the mental habits, including adjusting interpretations. Your mental dialogue is brimming with your knee-jerk interpretations of what happens in your life hour by hour.

Whenever an unpleasant event occurs, or anything that makes you feel uncomfortable, that's a trigger to stop and review what you are telling yourself. If you verbalize these thoughts to yourself or someone else, they are closer to the surface and easier to detect. With practice, you can more easily identify patterns. Many times, our thoughts are only feelings, not words. Try to tap into the feeling, put words on it, then work to change your interpretation.

For example, you've just given a report to your boss. The next time you pass her in the hall, she has a scowl on her face. Your stomach tightens. You notice this and attach anxiety to that feeling. Why are you anxious? You're assuming she didn't like your report. Stop and change your interpretations. There could be any number of things happening in her mind that could create that scowl.

Someone you know seems to snub or ignore you. You feel hurt, embarrassed. Stop and say to yourself, "He probably had something on his mind or didn't see me here."

We often make random comments to ourselves or others that may reflect our worldview and put us into a negative frame of mind. For example, "Well, it just figures that . . ." or "Seems like every time I . . ." These phrases, and whatever follows, reinforce the idea that the world is out to get you. "Every time I leave the house, it starts raining." Or "I always seem to pick the slowest grocery store line, even if it looks shortest to me." Have you ever said such things to yourself? They seem innocent, almost automatic, but reflect an underlying belief that the arbitrary elements of life are conspiring against you. Become aware of these thoughts. There is no organized plot to mess up your day or your life. Events are most often random and neutral, but you may *interpret* them as either good or bad.

Much of what lies behind such interpretations boils down to assumptions about the way life works. We may not know we have such assumptions. Assuming things will generally go wrong is bound to shade our view of life in a negative way and, of course, influence our interpretations. Albert Einstein once made the statement that one of the most important questions we can ask is whether we believe in a friendly universe. In other words, do we believe we exist in an atmosphere that is inclined toward our good, toward our success? Our answer to that question colors our approach and expectations to all of life.

As Christians, we can answer a resounding *yes* to this question, and it isn't based on wishful thinking or a helpful belief. It's based on what we know about God, that He *is* on our side causing all things to work together for good. (Romans 8:28). If this is our framework, we can more easily give a favorable interpretation to the events that come across our path. This doesn't absolve us of our responsibility, if we are the one who made a mistake, but even in that case, God can use it for good.

Or maybe you aren't sure whether the hard situation you're in is God's will for you for your refinement, your own mistake, or something else. You can acknowledge that God is still God and can do something good with the present situation. You trust Him, you do *your* part, and you keep an expectant attitude. If this is a difficult task, you may need to evaluate your view of God. Review passages of Scripture that speak of His attributes to remind you of His goodness.

Sometimes we have to *choose* how we think about God. Instead of saying to ourselves, "Where was God when this happened to me?", we can instead say, "God's ways are higher than mine, and He is good. I know He will use this, even though it was painful. He has a perfect plan and is still in control." What a difference the second interpretation will make in our emotions and outlook on life. *That is real faith lived out.*

You may have expectations related to other people, easily identifiable by the word "should": People should be more efficient. People should be kinder to their elders, to children, to neighbors, to customers. Sometimes we may behave indignantly to the violation of one of our "shoulds", which is merely our interpretation of the way things ought to be according to us. They block us from really understanding the person or situation because we've made up our minds in advance.

How about this list of "shoulds"? Do you identify with any of these?

- My parents should be willing to give me money regularly.
- My children should visit every weekend if they love me.
- My husband and children should recognize all I do for them. They're just selfish.
- The summer should be warmer. After all, the winter was really long!
- The customer service department should be more accommodating. They didn't even seem to care about my concerns, no matter how much I yelled!
- My colleagues should recognize how competent I am and respect me more.
- My wife/husband should know what I like without my telling her/him.
- I should have gotten a response from my friend by this time.
- They should do something about this!
- The government should make a law about this situation.

Stop for a moment. Be honest, if only to yourself and your journal. Do you believe any of these "shoulds"? If you believe any one of them and it is violated, you'd probably feel frustrated, yet you have created it *yourself* because of your belief in something that is not necessarily true.

But the world operates according to its own rules, not yours. Having a "should" is a way of blaming others for our discomfort or inconvenience. But does blaming others *really* make us feel better? Hopefully this section will show a better, more effective, and peaceful way to feel better. Our adherence to a list of "shoulds" is largely unconscious. As you tune in to your thoughts more and more, these beliefs can be identified and discarded.

This being said, some "shoulds" we have are really important, to safeguard our rights and safety and those of others. Maybe there is something you can and should do about it. If so, by all means, try to help the situation, instead of just grumbling about it, expecting people to either read your mind, or solve the problems you're concerned about.

Adjusting Your Interpretations

Adjusting your interpretations can rescue your emotions and maybe your whole day from a downward spiral. By choosing to look at a situation or an event through a different lens, one that gives a positive slant instead of assuming the worst, you open yourself up to a more positive outcome.

For example, failure is unpleasant. No one will argue with that. Yet, the way we interpret it shines an entirely different light on it. Failure gives us an opportunity to review our strengths and weaknesses, to learn what went wrong and why, then to take a different course of action. It opens new challenges and leads to personal growth.

Maybe your life situation seems negative right now. Perhaps you lost a job you liked and had to take one you don't like. You can interpret this as a horrible situation and continually remember how happy you used to be. Or you can see it as a passage to something better, a fill-in employment to pay the bills until you find a better job. The current less-than-ideal life is merely a time for proactive preparation for a great future. The situation hasn't changed, but the way you look at it has. Instead of marinating in your sad situation, you will feel more hopeful and forward-looking as you anticipate better times. Your positive thoughts create an interpretation of the event.

Is there something to learn from the situation, a way in which you can grow emotionally or spiritually? Is God lovingly trying to get your attention so that you can take steps that will lead to your good? Maybe you're on the wrong course and He is trying to help you avert disaster. Ask yourself, "What might God want to teach me or change through this situation?"

Here are some other examples of adjustment of interpretations:

When I got negative feedback on my report/project/performance, I felt bad at first. (normal human response) Then I became aware of some habitual weaknesses I have. (self-discovery) Now I can work on improving them. The feedback will help me do better. (positive response leading to personal growth and likelihood of doing better)

It's a shame I got sick and missed the Christmas party. (normal disappointment for missed pleasure) But at least I wasn't sick on the cruise we took. That would have been much worse. (seeing the disappointing event within a larger perspective, leading to gratitude instead of regret)

The break-up of that relationship was really hard for me. (normal emotions of rejection and hurt) But now I'm relieved I didn't go too far in a relationship that's not good for me. (realization that some temporary pain can prevent bigger disasters) Now that the hurt is fading, I can see things more clearly.

Changing your interpretation can also help prevent a potential argument or a ruined relationship. Interpreting the best possible scenario and attributing good motivations to other people will help us to believe the best. As we do this the other person usually responds better than if we'd expected the worst or assumed her bad intentions toward us. It's human nature to respond well to positive expectations. It's also true that when we think the worst, people often meet our expectations.

Interpretations may flow out of self-doubt. "She probably thinks I look unstylish." Or "they're all waiting for me to fall on my face." You *can't* read other peoples' minds. There's a high probability that the people in question are thinking of how *they* look, not you!

What about comparisons? A man takes lunch with his colleagues but is so busy comparing how much they earn compared to his measly salary, that he can't enjoy his food. Truthfully, he doesn't know much about their private lives, if they are happy, or what their journeys have been. He just feels inadequate by comparing himself. Jealousy poisons our interpretations for months or years, ruining time that we could have been thankful and productive. We can't compare one life to another one. We can only do our best with our *own* lives.

Adjusting your interpretations will help as you confront big problems as well as inconveniences or annoyances. After the following reflection questions, read about *Mind Frames* and see how to recognize and change yours.

Steps for the Journey

What are some frequent negative situations or interactions you encounter and what are your typical interpretations of those?

How can you change your interpretations?

Practice tuning into your feelings and thoughts as you go through your day. What do you find? Write these down on a notepad and find associations between feelings and mental dialogue. What is the dialogue? (You may need to put a feeling into a statement. For example, discomfort or embarrassment when someone ignores you. Identify embarrassment and shame.)

Change the dialogue in your mind for a given situation. What is the new dialogue?

Make a practice of doing this whenever it happens. It won't be automatic right away. Keep working at it to build this new mental habit.

What random comments do you often make to yourself? What do these reflect of your view of your life, and life in general?

How can the practice of viewing God as benevolent and powerful influence how you feel about your daily life?

Do you need to change your view of God? (Make a decision to do this.) If so, how will you change it? Are there Scriptures you can post, meditate on, or memorize to strengthen your view of God? Find at least 3 and post them somewhere you'll see them.

What are some "shoulds" you frequently hold to? What do these really mean for you? How can you change them or abandon them?

What is a situation that has bothered you for a while? You've thought of different interpretations. It still bothers you, even though you admit you aren't absolutely sure what happened.

Let it go. Are you willing to let go the painful or frustrating interpretation and admit that you simply aren't sure what really happened? This takes both humility and wisdom.

Practice the following phrases to yourself each time something similar happens: "I'm not sure what was really going on. It probably doesn't matter." You can even shrug for good measure! Or "I'm sure she had her own reasons that have nothing to do with me." Or "These employees have so much to do, they're bound to make mistakes once in a while."

If you get into the habit of explaining to yourself in this way, your tension will decrease, and you'll be more patient and gracious (and Christlike) with people.

This is a habit well worth developing. It will save you sadness, disputes with friends and loved ones and cranky moods. And it's what God wants for you. Let this sink in. He'll help you if you let Him.

You'll build the habit of giving a positive, neutral, or uncertain interpretation to small problems that erupt. This good habit will go with you during every season of your life.

Believe the best. The fruit of this will not only be increased peace, but better relationships with others. You'll have more peace inside, more confidence in yourself, and people will be more drawn to you. Best of all, you'll have a more positive outlook on your life, finding positive elements and stronger faith in even difficult seasons of life.

Day Nine

Making Mind Frames Work for You

Have you ever been in a dark mood, focused on a problem, sad or deeply depressed about it, in tears and unable to cope—then a few hours later you are laughing with friends and can't remember why you were so upset just a while ago? Have you been obsessed by worry over a person or situation? You're in a mind frame that is driven by negative thoughts to the point where you feel like it's controlling you. As the day unfolds, you enter a different frame far removed from those bad feelings.

Sometimes all it takes to create this change of mind frame is a different setting or activity. Imagine you are feeling sad as you drive or ride to work (idle waiting is a fertile ground for negative thoughts), but once you get there you become drawn into your job. An hour or so later, you realize you aren't sad anymore. You've been mentally preoccupied by something else, so it broke the strength of that negative emotion. Or you're frustrated about an event or a person, but after going out with friends, you realize it wasn't such a big deal.

Many factors contribute to a negative mind frame. Interpretations do this quicker than you can blink an eye. Lightning-fast negative interpretations of a discussion can raise your anger against another person. Scientists have discovered that our emotional mind, the part of our brains responsible for our emotions, reacts more quickly than the area that handles logic and reasoning. We are inclined to act impulsively on the emotion of the moment, but the rational thought process takes longer to sort it all out. That's why we regret emotional reactions or outbursts once we've had time to mull them over. And it's an excellent reason to pause before acting on that consuming feeling.

Sometimes we are simply in a cranky or tearful mood. We might know why, or we might not. Wouldn't it be nice to be able to push a pause button on that negative frame (like a movie frame), step neatly out of the box and into a better, more pleasant one, like the one you have when you're with friends? It takes some practice and isn't necessarily easy at first, especially if you have big pressures in your life. But you can learn to do it. Research has shown that the human being is capable of objectively observing his own thinking patterns, as though he steps outside of himself and looks down at them. Doing this pushes a pause button on your runaway emotions.

Just a word here on grieving. If you have lost loved one (or a loved situation, which can also trigger grieving), this feeling is *legitimate*. Experiencing it is healthy and part of your healing process. However, after some time has gone by, you may still be subject to periods or waves of sadness (and sometimes at inconvenient moments.) This is also true of a difficult breakup or loss of a close friendship. These painful emotions resulting from loss won't necessarily be due to a faulty interpretation, but they are painful, nonetheless. In that situation, too, you can practice a mind frame exercise. Doing so can take you from a sad state into a different one, which will help you manage those difficult emotions.

How does changing mind frames work? First, recognize when you're in a negative (angry, depressed, regretful, indignant, etc.) mind frame. Remind yourself that the emotions are strong now but will lessen in a little while. Imagine yourself pushing the pause button on a machine, only the machine is your mental frame. It freezes everything, every thought, every emotion.

While in the "frozen" state, you imagine yourself stepping physically out of the frame into a neutral hallway.

Remember the positive frame you had not so long ago. You want to leave the neutral hallway and return to the positive frame. Consider how you feel in that positive frame and what you are doing. Say aloud, "Lord, I'm giving these feelings to you." Give Him the pressure, the burden, and the negative feelings. Picture yourself placing them into a small boat and pushing the boat away from you out to His waiting arms. In 1 Peter 5:7 (NIV version), we read "Cast all your anxiety on him because he cares for you." This word 'cast' is not a passive gesture requiring no energy. When you cast something away from you, it's forceful, intentional. We need to use that kind of determination and energy to cast our anxiety, our daily problems, our regrets, and worries on Him. Give it all your strength as you push the boat of worries toward God for Him to handle.

It is essential at this point to change your activity. Go out on an errand. Clean out a closet. Start baking muffins and turn on some loud jazz or salsa music or anything upbeat that you like. See a movie or call a friend. If you're feeling overwhelmed and out of control, but can't change your activity, at least stop, and observe something in the room. Say aloud or in your mind, "What a nice color red that is. Is it more pink or more red . . ."? Or, "I wonder what kind of watch that girl is wearing. I may get myself one." It may sound silly, but this minor forced distraction will actually *interrupt* and lesson the negative flow of emotions.

Do whatever is helpful to pull yourself out of your negative state (as long as it isn't illegal or immoral!). *However, don't skip the step* (even if you do this later) of *evaluating* the interpretations that you need to change. Wait until your emotions have calmed and you're in a better place. Reflect on whatever interpretations or beliefs got you into that emotion-driven state. Question them. Are they true? What else could be affecting your response? Maybe there is an underlying or unrelated situation that is blowing your emotions out of proportion. Previous hurts? Background worry? Are you making it bigger than it should be because of other factors? Identify them.

You might have a problem that is truly hard. How are you facing it? As a catastrophe and you're helpless? Or as a challenge, and you've got what it takes?

Once out of the negative emotional state, your mind will be better able to function clearly and calmly, and that will make it easier to plan steps of action.

Steps for the Journey: Mind Frames

What are some negative mind frames you frequently visit? (Write the situation and corresponding interpretation).

How have your interpretations affected your emotions, getting you into a negative frame?

How else could you interpret the situation?

During an emotionally calm phase, mentally walk yourself through trying the mind frame exercise described above. Imagine yourself doing this. In what ways will you distract yourself from the emotion? What can you fix your attention on when this happens? What activity can you do to pull yourself into another mind frame?

When you have runaway emotions again, remember the "dress rehearsal" you did and try to do the same exercise to change your mind frame. Record how it works for you. How can you make this more effective?

List five things you can do to pull yourself out of a negative frame.

1.

2.

3.

4.

5.

In the space below, record your continued progress on recognizing, questioning, and changing your interpretations.

"I know the Lord is always with me. I will not be shaken, for he is right beside me. No wonder my heart is glad, and I rejoice. My body rests in safety." Psalm 16:8-9

Key Thought: Change your interpretation and you change your experience.

Habit Three:

The Habit of Self-Esteem

Day Ten

The Vital Importance of Self-Esteem

Healthy self-esteem is a mental habit that can literally alter the course of your life. Whether positive or negative, it is a powerful motor for a life of fulfillment or a life of disappointment. It should not be underestimated. Many times, when a person comes to Christ, this elevates his self-esteem to some extent. He understands himself to be a new creation—forgiven, purified, and surrounded by Christ's love. Yet, despite these precious blessings, he may still suffer from a lack of self-acceptance. The good news is that God accepts us through Christ. The bad news is that we don't accept ourselves, and it affects everything we do.

Therapist Nathaniel Branden, known as the father of the self-esteem movement, states in his book, *The Six Pillars of Self-Esteem*, "If self-esteem is the health of the mind, then few subjects are of comparable urgency. . . As the issue of self-esteem came more clearly into focus for me, I saw that it is a profound and powerful human need, essential to healthy adaptiveness, that is, to optimal functioning and self-fulfillment. To the extent that the need is frustrated, we suffer and are thwarted in our development." He points out that "Healthy self-esteem correlates with rationality, realism, intuitiveness, creativity, independence, flexibility, ability to manage change, willingness to admit (and correct) mistakes, benevolence, and cooperativeness." It is a predictor of personal happiness, according to a study done by D.G. Meyers in his book, *The Pursuit of Happiness*.

Do I Have Low Self-Esteem?

The idea of self-esteem sometimes gets a bad reputation. In fact, many Christians don't think healthy self-esteem is important. Not many Christian books exist on this topic. Many confuse it with self-focus, arrogance, or pride. It is none of these things. A positive self-esteem doesn't create qualities that aren't there. It includes self-acceptance, based on a realistic assessment of *who* you really are, including strengths *and* weaknesses, not what people have *told* you you are. It's not even what you may think of yourself because of unfortunate circumstances or poor choices you may have made. Everyone makes mistakes and bad decisions sometimes. They don't define you.

Trying to improve our self-esteem is no more selfish than taking vitamins, getting enough sleep, or exercising to improve your physical health. Let's rather think of self-esteem, as Dr. Branden suggests, as the "health of the mind." This puts self-esteem in an entirely different light and raises its importance for our overall well-being. God wants us healthy and healed in our view of ourselves. The apostle Paul urges us to be honest in our evaluation of ourselves. That means not higher than we are, nor lower. Just reality, who God has made us to be. (Romans 12:3)

We carry around varying degrees of deficient self-esteem. You may say, "What can I do about my self-esteem? It's because of my childhood and the things people told me all my life." Your background and life experiences may have created a foundation for a poor self-esteem, but self-esteem can be changed.

In addition to reading this book and working through the questions, there is more you can do. You can read other works about this subject, join a support group, see a counselor, or form a group of friends to work on this issue together, using this and other helpful books on the topic. (Dr. Nathaniel Branden has written several helpful books on self-esteem.) There are ways to be proactive, and no effort you take to improve your self-esteem will be wasted.

But... Aren't we Sinful?

In some churches we often hear about how sinful we are, how depraved, and unable to do anything good apart from God. Sometimes believers are encouraged to have a low view of themselves as if this is godly and humble. Is this the Biblical view? Does God want us to see ourselves (despite being redeemed by Christ) primarily as sinners? Here's a small sampling of what He thinks of us in Christ:

We are new creations (2 Corinthians 5:17)
We are pure and holy, freed from sin (1 Corinthians 1:30b)
Our sin natures were crucified. (Romans 6:6)
There is no condemnation for those who are in Christ. (Romans 8:1)

As we've read, a healthy self-esteem is essential to a healthy, happy life. Part of a healthy self-esteem is being thankful and accepting of the way God made you, just like you are. Know that, like a parent, He loves us without conditions. *"I have loved you, my people, with an everlasting love. With unfailing love, I have drawn you to myself."* Jeremiah 31:3.

It is important to distinguish what God's Word teaches from what it does *not* teach. It is true that in our human effort, we are unable to save ourselves because we have fallen short of God's requirement for salvation. We all need reconciliation with God through His grace shown to us through His Son Jesus Christ, a reconciliation we receive as a gift by faith.

This does not mean that apart from Christ we have no *value* or ability to do good. It does not mean we are completely worthless apart from Him or that we don't have talents, good impulses, and positive qualities. None of us would look around at other people and say they have no value. We know that they do, and so do we. So do *you*! At salvation we don't *receive* value that we didn't have before, because every created being has tremendous value, even those who don't have a relationship with God.

When we come to Christ, we receive a new nature and spiritual gifts, added to our natural giftedness. As our heart is regenerated and we begin a relationship with God, a new, spiritual dimension is added. The connection with God is made and His fellowship, power, and promises become available to us.

It does not glorify God when you consider yourself as nothing or inferior, or if you refuse to recognize your good qualities and focus on your mistakes or inabilities. You are His workmanship *before and after* your salvation. Then at the moment of your conversion, you *also* receive his spiritual blessings and gifts! There is *no* justification in Scripture for you to think of yourself as having no talents, no abilities, and no value apart from Christ.

Underneath negative wrong beliefs we may consciously or unconsciously carry around with us, there is a sensitive, loving person who wants to live the best life he or she possibly can, desiring to grow in Christ. Your job is to find that person, find the ways you yourself have been putting that person down, and begin to regard yourself in more positive, realistic, and Biblical terms.

We'll reflect more on this in the coming days, exploring how you can evaluate your self-esteem and raise it in a healthy, Biblical way. The following section begins that process, taking account of where you are now in your self-esteem.

Steps for the Journey

Answer the following honest questions.

How do you generally feel about yourself?

Do you feel adequate for life? Are you lacking in some ways?

Do you generally accept yourself the way you are, even with your needs for improvement?

Would you say you have low, medium, or high self-esteem? Is there room for improvement in this area?

How do you feel about the topic of self-esteem and improving it? (Guilty? Hopeful? Desperate to do so? Eager to get started?)

As you look more in depth at this area for the next few days, you'll likely have some insights into your life. *Take this very seriously*, since improving this habit is important for your future success.

Day Eleven

A Self-Esteem Assessment

Most of us have some degree of negative self-esteem. This may affect only specific areas, or it might be a pervasive attitude touching all of life. Many factors affect our self-esteem. The home we grew up in is often the first cause that comes to mind, but there could be other reasons or a combination of factors. As you read through the coming chapters, you'll start identifying sources of your self-esteem deficits. Even small amounts of lagging self-esteem can be improved, so don't minimize or skip this part if you feel it doesn't apply to you. The next chapter will give some more help in identifying the presence of low self-esteem.

Today's chapter will require some reflection and recall on your part. The following is an important step in discovering where your self-esteem is right now and how it might have been damaged at some point in your life. What you discover today will help you to apply the principles in the following chapters and in the entire book! *Don't skip this chapter.* It is foundational for your growth.

Turn to a clean page in your journal or notebook. Find a quiet place where you'll be undisturbed. Give this exercise at least 30 minutes. Later, once you've done this part, return to what you've written. Ask God to guide you in your reflection and remembering.

Part One

Reflect deeply about each period of your life. Take each part one at a time and remember what you can, both your *overall thoughts* as well as *significant events*. Be sure to include both general and specific memories for each phase of your life. Start with early and late childhood, then adolescence, then young adulthood. Include everything up to the present time.

Write a short paragraph about what you remember in each period, including positive and negative events and their impact on you. Don't stop to censor your thoughts or evaluate anything. Just write freely. When you are finished set this aside.

Later that day or the next day, go back to what you wrote and read it carefully. Note any patterns that may have affected how you view yourself. Did parents, teachers, or friends tell you things that stuck with you in a negative way (and may have even influenced how you behaved afterward), or were there events in your life that have left a black mark on your self-image? Write these down in detail.

How have you felt about yourself in those areas and overall since that time? What other observations do you want to write down and consider? Write freely whatever comes into your mind following this exercise.

Note any mistakes you have made as well as anything you are proud of. Did your mistakes have an influence on how you currently feel about yourself and your potential? Write these things down and how they affected you.

Tell yourself you did the best you could at the time. The results might have been quite positive or not so great. *Every* life includes both and yours does too. Your brain may acknowledge God's forgiveness, but you won't fully receive it until you forgive yourself too. Picture yourself giving yourself a big hug of acceptance and forgiveness.

Maybe you have negative messages running through your mind, but you aren't sure where they come from. As you re-read your life story, do you see any patterns that may have triggered these negative messages or images? Write them down.

Once you have identified some of the causes of your negative self-image, you'll have a place to start working on it. This will be a process. At certain points in that process, you'll notice accusations you're holding onto in your mind that you need to refute. Write them down. Identifying wrong beliefs we've held onto for a long time is a powerful and vital step toward changing them. Mentally take them to court and cross-examine them.

Take some time now to write a phrase to refute each negative belief about yourself. For example, "You're not very smart, are you?" spoken by an admired adult can create a scar that never heals. Refute it and turn it into an affirmation. "I am at least as smart as everyone I know, or smarter," or "I'm more gifted in science (or art, or languages, or math) than anyone I know." Continue refuting all your negative messages, replacing them with positive affirmations. Then re-read the positive affirmations (never the negative ones) daily.

Part Two

Write out a list of all your strengths. You may have difficulty with this at first. Many people do. Write what comes to mind, or what people have told you. Leave plenty of space below this list because additional thoughts will come to your mind, and you can add them later. Be honest with your strengths.

Write a list of your weaknesses. Don't exaggerate them, and don't use derogatory words for yourself. They will be part of the tapestry that is your view of yourself. Work on these and try to change some of them, but for now you're just recognizing what they are.

Think of one person without weaknesses. You'll find there aren't any. Embrace the weaknesses you identified. Of course, you'll want to change them if you can, and you should try to improve them, but don't beat yourself up for them. Imagine buying a home you really like. You know it needs new paint inside and a new kitchen and heating system, but the strengths and overall value outweigh the weaknesses. Besides that, you'll see the potential of it renovated. Imagine *you* are that house. Overall, you're fantastic and of great value to God. But you have a few renovations to do, and with time you'll do them. Focus on your strengths and overall value. And don't forget, God will help you with the renovations!

What effect has your conversion had on your self-esteem? Has this been positive or negative? Do you see in yourself any of the following images? As a redeemed child of God? As a prince or princess, heir to God's kingdom? Favored and forgiven by God Himself?

Or do you see yourself as a filthy sinner saved by grace, but sitting on the back porch of heaven? Always falling short of God's perfect standard? Notice your emotional response as you read the previous phrases. What does that tell you?

Which image accurately reflects God's grace and love for us, based on His Word? How can you revise your images of your relationship to God, if needed? Make sure your image is based on His truth and transformation of your life.

What is the general atmosphere of the church you attend? Is there a lot of emphasis on sin and falling short? Is low self-esteem prized as a virtue? How much emphasis is there on God's grace and forgiveness?

Do you think God values you just as you are, as a human being He created, with all of your qualities and weaknesses? Does He accept you? What are you reasons for your beliefs? (Are they Biblical?)

Write out a short summary of the factors that have negatively affected your self-esteem during your life. In other words, what have you learned, realized, or remembered about yourself?

How might your life could be different if you improved those negative beliefs and thoughts about yourself?

What do you think God wants for you in this area of your life?

Read the following Scriptures to learn more about how God wants to empower you to improve your life.

Philippians 2:13

Philippians 1:6

Philippians 3:12

Jeremiah 18:3-6

"O Lord, you have examined my heart and know everything about me...You saw me before I was born. Every day of my life was recorded in your book...How precious are

your thoughts about me, O God. They cannot be numbered!"
Psalm 139:1, 16-17

Day Twelve

Transforming Self-Esteem

If any hurtful messages from the past have damaged your view of yourself, you owe it to yourself to attack these head-on. But a lifetime of harmful messages doesn't get reprogrammed overnight. It will take persistence, like the patient rerouting of a stream that has dug a gully in the earth. But it can be done.

Psychologist Matthew McKay points out in his helpful book, *Self-Esteem*, that circumstances are only indirectly related to self-esteem. One factor that weighs even more is our *thoughts*. He is speaking of a mental habit so pervasive it directs our lives. That's a habit worth changing, important enough to merit your deliberate concentration.

You probably know several people (possibly yourself included) who have negative thoughts about themselves, despite their new identity in Christ. How often do you fall into the following traps?

- Comparing yourself negatively to someone else—whether your friends, co-workers, or even total strangers. This could be in the area of appearance, career or personality traits. Most often this is done in a quiet, mental evaluation where you come up lacking.

- Negative self-talk. Sometimes we talk to ourselves in a way that we'd never talk to another person, nor permit another person to talk to us. Yet, we often do this subconsciously, and sometimes even consciously. Have you ever called yourself an unkind name aloud, after doing something careless? You might doubt there's an impact, but it has more than you think. (It also contradicts what God says about us!)

- Unrealistic expectations. Maybe you are trying to please an impossible-to-please parent, teacher, boss or significant other. Maybe *you're* the one who is impossible to please. Your standards may be too high, and you don't give yourself any margin for human mistakes, fatigue, or poor judgment. Maybe you are trying to 'be like Christ' to the point of not accepting who and where you are *now*, on your unique spiritual journey.

- Using destructive images or labels for yourself. For example, do you have a label or image of yourself as a loser, a slob, marginal, unlucky, inept, or alone? Find the negative label that you most often use with yourself. If there is a mental picture associated with it, it's even more destructive. Where does this come from? Other people? Does it go so far back you can't remember where it came from? Cross examine it, as if you were in a courtroom. What makes you believe it is it true? What is your evidence and how reliable is it? These labels and images must be ripped from your thoughts and replaced with kinder, more accurate labels. If you are consciously loving and compassionate with yourself, this will gradually affect your self-esteem as well. Instead of 'weird', you could call yourself 'unique.' Adopt new words for yourself. What about one of these: princess, pioneer, champion, gifted, solid, artist, wise, compassionate, a blessing?

In your childhood or adolescence, you might have heard negative messages about yourself that were either verbal or non-verbal. Maybe the verbal message was "my problems are all your fault," or "you always screw up." These messages leave deep wounds. Or maybe you had parents who were often preoccupied and too busy to pay attention to you, so you heard a nonverbal message that said, "You don't matter. You're unimportant." This is just as damaging and can have lasting effects. Long after the messages stop, you continue to believe them, whether consciously or subconsciously.

This process of accumulating and reinforcing messages covers a period of years, to the point that they become your reality. You may not even be aware of them. Just as it has taken years to program the negative messages into your mind, it will take deliberate effort to reprogram your thoughts. One tool that will help you do this is positive affirmations. An affirmation is a positive statement of truth, such as "I am a worthwhile person," or "I love and accept myself."

At first you may feel silly stating affirmations, but with time the new, positive messages will begin to push out the negative thoughts, retraining them. There won't be any more room for the negative ideas. A new habit will form, and you will truly believe the positive statements. This will transform your view of yourself.

Author Melodie Beattie speaks strongly about the power that each one of us has to change our own messages and beliefs through affirmations, in her book *Codependent No More*. She states that affirmations aren't just wishful thinking, but rather our response to the negative programming we have received all our lives. Deliberate effort must be applied to these deeply entrenched messages which silently control us. Affirmations are a concrete way we take hold of the negative messages and reroute them by building new, healthy mental habits.

Christians benefit from practicing affirmations. Start first with faith-neutral affirmations, ones that focus on you as a *person*, not (yet) on you as a Christian person. This initial step will affirm you in your *self*, and this is a good place to start. Why? Because your faulty self-esteem is a deep layer that may block your ability to assimilate spiritual truths. Neutral affirmations will focus on *your* qualities as a person. Then later, you will add spiritual affirmations for subsequent layers of emotional strength. Biblical affirmations focus more on God's qualities and the changes He has made in you. These are important too, of course, but the weakness is in *your* self-esteem, so this is where you should start.

Maybe you like the idea of affirmations, but don't know what you would affirm. That's where many of us get stuck. Later, you'll be asked to identify some of your negative messages. After doing this, you'll consider how to make a statement that reflects the opposite. That's a great way to make an affirmation. If one of your negative messages is, "I'm barely getting by," change it to "I can do anything I set my mind to." The message, "I'm so fragile and weak," becomes "I'm full of strength and energy." Say them to yourself, even if you don't really believe them yet. Contrary to what you may expect, they will begin to take root in your subconscious and change your thought patterns.

Make a list of several affirmations that fit for you, that is, statements you *want* to be true about you. Borrow other helpful phrases from books. Use certain affirmations for a while, then swap them out for others.

These positive statements aren't prideful. Remember the goal is to lift a low self-esteem, so that you see yourself the way God sees you. It isn't wrong to accept yourself or approve of yourself. Another way to create affirmations for yourself is to look back at the exercise where you listed your strengths. Use some of these as affirmations.

Here are some ideas for more affirmations:

- I accept and approve of myself.
- I'm God's unique creation.
- I'm full of talents and abilities and I will succeed.
- I'm loveable and valuable.
- I'm as good as anyone else.
- The past is over. I am at peace.
- I am safe. God is with me.
- I deserve to rejoice in life. I will rejoice in life.
- I am a loving friend to myself.

What if you don't yet believe the affirmation? The goal is to *reprogram* your negative thoughts. These statements won't be untrue for very long. Soon they will be your new truth if you keep at it until the new habits are formed and the negatives are pushed out.

Once the truth of the above statements is well-anchored in your mind and you feel your self-esteem regarding your *human self* getting stronger, add some Biblically based affirmations. Here are some of them, based on Scripture verses, though you'll want to add your favorites. Put them in your own words to give them a greater impact on your heart.

- God knows and loves me completely just as I am.
- He has loved me since eternity past.
- Nothing will ever stop God from loving me.
- Christ gives me strength to do what I need to do.

An important note: If you have been abused or have experienced other tragic events in your life, you should seriously consider consulting a professional counselor. If you aren't sure, do it anyway. Don't take chances with your emotional health and future.

When I came back from France with my life, marriage, and faith in tatters, I needed emotional and spiritual restoration. One day I heard about a devotional book that I now know is used and loved by many people, called *Jesus Calling*. This book played a part in my emotional healing, and not only because of the beautiful devotional writings for each day. Each devotional is accompanied by two or three Scriptures. As I read the verses, I was struck over and over how much love God pours out on us, how much He seeks us, and how many promises He makes to us. Little by little, I was healed by His love. Don't neglect this vital truth: God's love heals us in many ways. Let Him heal your self-esteem, let Him bring restoration to any part of your life that needs to be healed, restored, or revived. Allow Him into every part of your learning and change process. He is the Healer and the satisfier of your soul, even the broken parts.

Steps for the Journey

<u>Try Affirmations</u>. Give them a try, even if you are a doubter. Try two or three affirmations, repeating them several times each day in the silence of your mind or as you get ready in the morning. If you read them regularly, they will change the way you feel about yourself. Changes will gradually occur in the way you see yourself. In fact, the first few times you may feel awkward, but keep going. Take ideas from your list of strengths. Refer to the examples and borrow some, as well as create your own to add to the list. (Here are some more to get you started.)

> I am worthy of the best life has to offer. (Remember your value as God's creation.)
> I am not helpless.
> I am loveable just as I am.
> God loves me just as I am.
> I don't have to impress anyone.
> I am satisfied with the person that I am.

Read the above list of affirmations and your list of strengths each day before you leave home or sometime early in the day. Do this every day. Try it and see what happens. Write down any observations of positive change in your journal. After using affirmations for at least three weeks, add some Scriptural affirmations, such as "I am God's beloved child," or "God loves me unconditionally. He calls me valuable and precious."

<u>Guard your thoughts</u>. Be aware of your daily thought patterns. This is where the battle will be won or lost. Keep your thoughts pointed in a true, positive direction and stay the course. Don't neglect this,

letting your thoughts be sucked back into the black hole of negativity. By this time, you have identified and hopefully debunked those negative statements about yourself. You'll slip once in a while, but don't go back to them in a regular way. Building a habit of thought takes time. <u>Read your positive statements each day for three weeks, minimum.</u> Record observations in your journal.

<u>Feed your mind the right foods</u>. Continue to fill your mind with positive information, inspiring reading, self-help, and encouraging books. Surround yourself with positive people. Identify the negative complainers and spend less time with them. (Don't *be* one either!) What will you read to encourage positive thoughts? What kind of people you spend time with? What other changes can you make to gradually turn your self-esteem around? Record your ideas, then be intentional.

<u>Jot notes in your journal about patterns you still struggle with</u>. Pay special attention to your negative self-talk and replace those negative statements. Don't let your journal be far from your reach. Review what you are learning on a regular basis and record your victories. Record positive changes and put a date on them. When you get discouraged, reread your progress, and renew your determination to reject the negative messages.

<u>Ask yourself the following questions</u>. Reflect honestly about your answers and record them in your private journal.

How do I feel about myself at the start of this process? What do I struggle with?

One month later (record the date): What changes have I seen in my self-esteem?

Three months later (record the date): What is my self-esteem like right now? What changes have occurred?

How has using affirmations affected my thought process and my emotions?

How has having a higher self-esteem changed things in my life for the better? Write down the positive results you've seen in the way you feel about yourself, the way you interact with others, or circumstances that have changed for the better as a result of improved self-esteem.

What can I do to maintain my self-esteem? Make a specific plan for what you'll think about and/or what influences you'll allow into your life to maintain what you've gained in more positive self-esteem. Again, be intentional. This is crucial, because you won't just drift into a better self-esteem without effort.

Day Thirteen

Continuing the Self-Esteem Journey

If you have tried the suggestions in the previous chapters in a serious way, you have seen positive changes in your self-esteem. But there is *more you can do*. It will be a lifelong process. Here are additional action steps that will support your new way of thinking as you grow, learn, and transform your thought patterns about yourself.

Live a life of purpose: Be a person who always has one or more goals you are working on at all times. Consider what you'd like to be, do, or have and make a goal out of it. You'll feel better about yourself as you move the needle in achieving your desires. Maybe it's getting a degree, a new job, a new house. Maybe it's working on a weakness. A goal can be anything you want. If you're not sure how to start, do the following: 1) Decide what you want (or what you don't want any more). 2) Determine what is stopping you from having what you want. 3) Make a list of steps and take one step at a time. Make sure it's something that *you* can do, not something based on another person's actions. It should be realistic, measurable, and specific. Example: 'Lose 5 pounds in the next 2 months' is more measurable and specific than 'Lose weight'. Set a deadline and evaluate your progress.

Don't be a victim. In *Six Pillars of Self-Esteem*, Dr. Nathaniel Branden lists the importance of self-responsibility. If you live life as a victim, expecting people and circumstances to make you feel better about yourself, you probably never will. You must take full responsibility for your current self-esteem. Maybe you were wronged in the past, but the present is your responsibility. That's good news because you can change this. *You* have the control in this area, and God wants you to take it. If you currently believe lies about yourself, you're the only one who can change that.

Don't ever underestimate your own competence. You have areas that you are good at. Know what they are. Areas of interest can become areas of competence, with study and preparation. Develop yourself. Always be improving your abilities. Always be growing.

Be a pipeline of love. As you learn to accept yourself more, you are more able to extend love and acceptance to others. Some days it will flow naturally. You know you are valuable, but you know the people around you, whatever they struggle with, are too. Be a pipeline of love, patience, and acceptance to others. Icing on the cake: love will come back to you as well.

Visualize how you want your life to be. Write it out in a paragraph in the present tense, as if it is already true. Include your personality qualities, situation, even appearance. Read this from time to time to remind yourself of what you want for your life, how you want to become. Commit this to prayer. Then act like that person, or *step into* that person even now, with the character and personality qualities you want to have, and gradually it will come to pass.

Be kind to yourself. That doesn't mean you shouldn't hold yourself to a high standard of behavior, morality, or work. You *should* keep up your standards and seek to improve every day. However, take time to treat yourself once in a while and remind yourself you are worth that effort. Remind yourself you are valuable and practice compassion with yourself.

You *are* valuable (God says so!) and you may be the last person who knows about it. It's time to start steering this ship of your self-concept in a new direction. It will alter the course of your journey.

Steps for the Journey

Look back at each of the above helpful principles for continuing the journey of transforming your self-esteem. For each one, decide on a step of action you will take for your life.

Take some time to consider your identity in Jesus Christ. As a believer, you have a new identity. Meditate on the following truths about who you are as a child of God.

"For we are God's masterpiece. He has created us anew in Christ Jesus, so we can do the good things he planned for us long ago." Ephesians 2:10

"Since we have been united with him in his death, we will also be raised to life as he was. We know that our old sinful selves were crucified with Christ so that sin might lose its power in our lives. We are no longer slaves to sin." Romans 6:5-6

"So you also are complete through your union with Christ, who is the head over every ruler and authority." Colossians 2:10

"This means that anyone who belongs to Christ is a new person. The old life is gone; a new life has begun!" 2 Corinthians 5:17

"So you have not received a spirit that makes you fearful slaves. Instead, you received God's Spirit when he adopted you as his own children. Now we call him, "Abba, Father." For his Spirit joins with our spirit to affirm that we are God's children." Romans 8:15-16.

Key Thought: Your self-esteem can be changed. It isn't selfish to try to improve it!

Habit Four

The Habit of Living in the Present

Day Fourteen

Definitions and Distractions

The mental habit of living in the present will enable you to squeeze the most out of your life every day.

Wait, don't we already live in the present? Technically, we do live in the present. But mentally, where do we live? Do our thoughts sweep us away to the future, the past, or some hypothetical realm for a large percentage of our hours? How much do we struggle with distraction?

Living in the present doesn't simply mean "stopping to smell the roses." As important as it is to enjoy the little things all around us, living in the present involves much more. It means living *consciously*. As we are conscious, we are more in touch with the ways we interact with the world around us, with others, with God, and with ourselves. How often do we go through our days on autopilot, barely observing anything around us until the day is over? Then we look back and we aren't sure whether or not it was a day well-spent.

In *The Art of Living Consciously,* Nathaniel Branden explains that living consciously means mentally engaging in all the things that concern us in our daily lives. Being active rather than passive in the moments that matter. It also means being willing to face facts, even if they aren't pleasant. It means being ready to correct our mistakes, and to seek learning and understanding as a habit of life. It means taking the time to reflect and evaluate what we experience.

Another advantage of living in the present is being better able to stay in touch with God throughout the day and hear what He wants to tell us. We'll be more alert to opportunities either to help or encourage someone else or take advantage of an opportunity that comes our way. In the words of the apostle Paul, "Be careful how you live. Don't live like fools, but like those who are wise. Make the most of every opportunity in these evil days." Ephesians 5:15-16. Though he is referring to living out our faith for God's glory, living consciously and mindfully is the best way to be conscious and receptive of everything that unique day has to offer.

The Power of the Present

It takes focused discipline to live in the present, since so many things clamor for our attention. In our times, it is probably harder than ever to live in the moment. Since advertising, technology, and social media have become such a huge part of our daily lives, mentally living in the physical, non-virtual world is a challenge. Aside from this, we may struggle with the past, mulling over regrets, or we might be knotted up with uncertainty about the future. There are many ways, (most of them counterproductive) to be drawn away from the present.

It has been said that our real home is here and now. For us, this fact exists in parallel with the truth of our eternal home. This is not only a promise, but a current reality that undergirds and guides the now. In a very real sense, we live in two dimensions, earthly and heavenly.

If we think of our lives as a journey, we realize that God entrusts our time on earth to us as stewards. Therefore, living consciously and mindfully is the only way that makes sense for a fully lived life on track with His will *and* our dreams. The present is reserved for living and doing. You can remember the past and anticipate the future, but you can only *live* in the present. You won't pass this way again. The things you can enjoy now, initiate, and complete now, risk now, will be the source of your future memories as well as your future results. Building quality into a relationship *now* will lead to a more rewarding and enjoyable one later. Choosing *now* how to live yields to a more productive and satisfying future. Along with that, what you enjoy and savor *now* will give more richness to your life. This is especially important if you are going through a season which is difficult or uninspiring. It will give balance to the bleak moments.

Steps for the Journey

How are you doing at living in the present? (Be honest . . .)

What factors make it difficult for you?

What are some of your habits that give clues that you might have difficulty in this area?

Is there an area where you need to do more or do better? If you haven't done it, what barriers exist, either inside you or outside? What are steps you can take this week to improve in this area?

List a few things to help you strengthen your view of God's care over your daily life. Find verses about His love and power and tape them to a mirror. Pray with a friend. Ask Him to help you trust Him more with your fears.

Make a list of what is positive in the present in your life. (And thank God for them!)

What are some opportunities you have today that you may not have in the future? (People, work opportunities, leisure, travel, etc.)

List some simple things that are yours to enjoy every day, as you drive or ride to work, as you walk in your neighborhood, visit friends and family, or enjoy your favorite hobbies or sports.

How can living in the present with heightened consciousness help you tune into God's direction for you?

How can this habit help you accomplish some of your goals in your life?

Day Fifteen

The Intrusion of the Past

Sometimes the past casts shadows on the present, making it harder to work on this habit. Regrets, guilt, a traumatic event, the rupture of a relationship, a bad decision, a lost loved one . . . all of these pull us toward unhappy thoughts, quickly followed by unhappy feelings. Nothing is gained by dwelling on the past *unless* you also learn something valuable from the situation. What could you have done differently, and how would you now act in a similar situation? Have you changed in a positive way, become softer and more humble, wiser, more determined to check the facts before jumping, because of something you suffered in the past?

If you made a wrong decision along the way, you can make it right, with God's help. That is, do the right thing with what you have, given what you have to work with. He is big enough to turn the situation around, despite our missteps.

Bitterness and grudges are sure ways to make ourselves miserable. Bitterness can even lead to health problems, lack of sleep, and a hard-edged personality that ends up pushing people away. It'll poison the best moments of our present *and* our future. You aren't getting back at the other person by continuing to feel bitter. You aren't *showing* them. You are only hurting yourself, as well as grieving God. If possible, reach out to the person who hurt you and talk it over or write a letter (even if there's no response) explaining how you felt about the incident. If that's not possible, decide you'll forgive, because that's what God wants and because it's healing for you. Let it go, whether it's a serious betrayal or a smaller offense you have a hard time shaking off. Shake it *now*. Hand it over to God. He'll help you do this. Of course, you won't magically forget about the incident. But if you choose to let that person (or entity) off the hook, it will set *you* free.

There are other issues that draw our attention and emotions from the past into the present, staining the current moments with negativity. Some are legitimate, such as grieving. Some are minor slights or comments. A negative past event such as missing out on a job promotion or a position you wanted is a source of unpleasant feelings as your mind goes backward. You wonder why *you* didn't get that job or promotion, and you allow frustration to take root. You could do the same thing with a relationship you wanted, but the other person didn't feel the same way. Or a friendship drifted apart or fell out, despite your efforts to repair it. There is no point and no benefit in dwelling on these things. They are part of your past life and whether you feel you did your best or not, they are over. Fix your mind present and ahead, not behind.

The future is like an unopened present God has in store for you. Part of the pleasure is in the surprise, like a Christmas present. If you think of the future in this way, it takes your mind off the past. This shift of thinking has its roots in your belief about God's goodness. Do you believe He's lovingly sovereign over your life, regardless of these uncomfortable events life throws at you or mistakes you may have made?

And what about guilt? You've likely heard this in your church or from a Christian friend or pastor, but here's a reminder: For legitimate guilt, confess it to God and ask His forgiveness. Do what you can to make amends, then let it go. Then there is false guilt, which is harder to detect since it masquerades as real guilt. Pray about this first. If you're still unsure of the nature of your guilt, take the time to talk to someone, a friend or a counselor, about it. An outside perspective can help you see if you need to make amends or if you're just beating yourself up over something that wasn't your fault. Whether the guilt is false or justified, if you're a believer, God has taken care of your guilt at the cross. He gives you complete cleansing and renewal. But you'll only benefit from that wonderful gift if you believe it and receive it. It is your birthright as a child of

God. But He has done His part in offering the gift. Your part is to receive it and have the burden lifted from your life. His forgiveness and peace are yours for the asking.

Do the same with any burdens from the past that weigh you down. Present them to your Heavenly Father. Transfer all that deadweight from your shoulders to His. He invites you but doesn't force you. But the freedom you'll experience when you do will enable you to live in the present with greater joy and lightness of step.

"Give all your worries and cares to God, for he cares about you." I Peter 5:7

Steps for the Journey

Do you tend to dwell on the past, regret past events or decisions? If so, what are the issues you focus on?

What effect has this had on you?

Has this affected your attitude about your life and/or opportunities?

Are you bitter or unforgiving toward another person or people? If so, who?

What negative results have shown up in your life from not forgiving that person? Have you gained anything from not forgiving?

Are you willing to forgive that person in order to free yourself (and be obedient to God)?

Is there anything you need to let go of? A regret from the past, whether something you did, or something done to you, a missed opportunity, or a grudge against someone? Write these on a piece of paper. Take the paper and throw it away, burn it, or bury it somewhere in your yard or in the sand. Concentrate on releasing these memories and emotions as you separate your life from that piece of paper. Record your feelings and the date you did this.

Release these matters into God's hands and ask Him to keep these things far from your mind. They will come occasionally, though, so have a strategy to break off the thought before it takes over your mind and emotions.

Day Sixteen

Worry and the Future Trap

Worry affects many people, and there are different kinds of worry. Often, people don't even realize they're worrying. They may have a vague sense of formless anxiety, sure that something disastrous will happen, though nothing they can put their finger on. This feeling can arise from a chaotic upbringing, when nothing ever seemed very certain or predictable, and this carries into adulthood. Or it may come from the knowledge that you're neglecting things (relationships, health, job performance), and sooner or later consequences will come due in an unpleasant way.

People also have specific worries about an event coming up, about the safety of loved ones, about finances, health . . . you name it. No argument, these are difficult issues to let go of. We may believe, consciously or not, that by worrying about the future, this will magically prevent the thing we dread from happening, or that by worrying we're *doing* something about a situation we otherwise have no control over. Consciously we know better. Depending on the situation, being prepared with a contingency plan will allow you to set aside the concern and be less plagued by the "what ifs" of life. But so many things in our lives are beyond our control. How does our faith in God affect our response to these things? Does it make enough of a difference?

Consider these beloved words from Jeremiah 29:11. "For I know the plans I have for you," says the Lord. "They are plans for good and not for disaster, to give you a future and a hope." Do we really believe that God holds us and our futures in His hands? If this is hard for you to believe, why is that the case? Maybe you have some unresolved hurt from your past that is leaking into the present, making it hard to trust God's goodness.

It is vital to keep in touch with our view of God. That means often bringing to mind His character and His promises. You might be surprised by your *real* view of God. Do you view Him as unconcerned about you? Powerless to keep His promises? Now is the time to identify what you truly believe about God's character and commitment to you as His child. It's also time to ask yourself, do you *really* believe His promises? Do you truly trust in His character? How should God's promises and character affect your worries about the future? Won't He carry you, whatever happens?

It's possible that this negative habit of worry is believed to be a positive quality. Imagine that a woman worries obsessively about her children every time they go out. She pictures herself as a dedicated mother and, in her definition, dedicated mothers worry. Therefore, she considers this normal and good. But is worry a necessary element of being a dedicated mother? Where does faith in God's protection come in, belief in His sovereignty? (Not to mention what the Bible says against worry.) Philippians 4:6

Michel de Montaigne, a French statesman and essayist from the 16th century said, "My life has been full of terrible misfortunes, most of which never happened." Does this describe you too, at least in your mental tendencies?

Another way to lose the present to the future is in planning too much for it. We get so embroiled in the five-year plan, the week's agenda, and the daily to-do list that we don't live in the present. It's *wise* to make goals and plans for the future, especially if you want to accomplish what's important to you. But consider how much mental energy you spend in the realm of the virtual world of future ideas and plans. As we do this, do we by-pass the present and its opportunities as well as simple pleasures by over-planning the future? Is it simply a way we try to control the future to protect ourselves?

Keep making goals and plans for your future, but don't let them be your main source of contentment and security or the realm in which you most often live. We so often spend more time preparing for life than living it. Thomas Carlyle, a Scottish philosopher, once said, "Our main business is not to see what lies dimly at a distance, but to do what lies clearly at hand." As we focus on the present and do our best within that realm, trusting God's promise to guide us day by day, the future (and the many things we worry about) will, in most cases, take care of itself. He has promised to guide us along the best pathway for our lives, advising and watching over us. (Psalm 32:8; Psalm 37:5, 23-4)

Do what you can to prepare for the future. And what you can't control, remember these words, "Give all your worries and cares to God, for he cares about you." 1 Peter 5:7

Dale Carnegie, well-known for his books and lectures on public speaking and interpersonal skills, in his excellent book, *How to Stop Worrying and Start Living* (published in 1948 but just as helpful, or even more so today), points out that the best way to prepare for the future is to use all our abilities on doing our best *today*. He adds that we often say, 'when I grow up,' 'when I retire,' or 'when I get married,' and focus on that future blissful circumstance, losing the chance to savor and fully live in the now. By doing our best in the current moment, we are, in fact, preparing for the future.

In Philippians 4:4, we read, "Don't worry about anything; instead, pray about everything. Tell God what you need and thank him for all he has done. Then you will experience God's peace, which exceeds anything we can understand." This is God's prescription for worry, and how often we do everything *but* what He has suggested. No wonder we lack His peace.

What's interesting is the phrase that comes immediately *after* this exhortation in verse 8. It says, "And now . . . fix your thoughts on what is true, and honorable, and right, and pure, and lovely, and admirable. Think about things that are excellent and worthy of praise." We're told not to worry, but then given a positive action to do instead. Don't just remove the worry and assume it will stay away. *Replace* it with the kinds of thoughts described in verse 8.

How do we shake off the hold of the past and future? By enjoying what we should: good memories from the past and anticipation of good things in the future. These two realms aren't made up of only regretful memories or frightening possibilities. Remember God's goodness. There are good memories to savor and good events to anticipate. For the past, learn what you can from a hurtful event then let it go. For the future, do what you can to prepare then release the rest to God's care. Don't waste the present, letting these thoughts of past and future crowd your mind, when there is so much potential for today, so much to do now. Your thoughts will be clearer and sharper if you keep the other 'time zones' in their own sealed compartments where they belong.

Living in *Real Time*

In recent years the term *real time* has been applied to many areas, specifically in computing and media. It may refer to something that occurs immediately, or else something that functions at the same speed as a real event would. To borrow, and perhaps distort the term, real time in your life is *now* time. It is occurring now— no taping, no delays, no repeats. Just reality. Your one chance to live this time and this experience. Moment by moment you can decide to live it in the best way possible, enjoying, giving, and achieving. Raise your awareness of now, making it conscious. And don't forget to enjoy the simple treasures as they quickly pass by.

Steps for the Journey

Do you feel dread or anxiety for the future? Do you picture the worst? What is your fear? What is so bad about this? Is there anything you can do now to plan for this, just in case, then release it? Write your plan.

Do you have difficulty trusting God with your future? Why might that be the case? Write out some reasons.

Take time to read the following verses from the Bible. They all affirm God's guidance of each one of His children. Write a one-sentence summary of each one and refer to them often.

Isaiah 48:17

Psalm 138:8

Jeremiah 29:11

Psalm 139:16

Psalm 32:8

Psalm 16:7-8

John 10:27

Isaiah 30:21

How much time do you spend planning for the future and anticipating it? Is it too much? How can you balance this?

Stop to notice what is around you. Develop your sense of observation. Too often we walk right by a beautiful or noteworthy scene. Don't get lost in your head and miss what is happening. The French have an expression, "passer à côté," which conveys the idea of overlooking something, but literally means "walk next to" without noticing. How many things do you walk right by every day without seeing or enjoying them? Write a list of all you notice once you make the effort to *see*.

Living in the present doesn't only pertain to enjoying the things around you. It also means full focus on the things that are important to you. What about your work? Are you doing your best, living in the present, giving full value to your job? Suppose you hate your job and find it difficult to do this. How active are you in pursuing a better situation that will make you more content and validate your talents and experience? Making these efforts in the present will change the outcome of your future.

What about your close relationships? Are you the proverbial parent who doesn't spend enough time with the kids or listen when they want to tell you something, or when they are going through a tough period in their lives? Do you appreciate the moments when they're still at home? Are you spending enough quality time with your spouse? List any changes you'd like to make in this area. Be specific.

Are there relationships that need to be repaired, that you have let go long enough? Are there people who need to hear how much you care about them, love them, respect them, and think they are good people? Are there words of encouragement that could be said in the present that you have put off saying until a more convenient time? List the names of these people and write what you'd like to say to them. Then plan a time when you can tell them in person or in a letter.

When you speak to someone, stay focused on that person. Ask a question. Then really listen to the answer. They'll be blessed by the attention you gave them, and the relationship will be enriched and strengthened. Try this with people you're meeting for the first time, people you've known for a while, casual acquaintances, and significant others. How did this make you feel? Record any observations and changes you plan to make.

Try this exercise

In the morning set aside 5 minutes. Sit still in a chair. Feel your toes, feel your legs, arms, fingers, all the way up. Concentrate on your body and the fact that it is there. Hear your breath, feel it. Take deep breaths and feel the air coming and going inside you. Think of how healthy you feel.

Look around the room you are in. Notice everything. Where did the objects come from? What does everything look like? What kind of light is coming through the window if there is one? Cloudy? Sunny? Rainy?

Then think of the day ahead and note the date. Remind yourself that this date will never again occur in history. What is going to happen today which will (or may) never happen again? What circumstances won't happen, except for today? If this is a difficult question to answer, check in at several points throughout the day, taking note as you go along. This day won't happen again.

Take a moment to be thankful for what is there, big and small. What you see, what you have (your health, your job, your family, your significant other, your car, your upcoming vacation), what you don't have (a disease, a financial problem, a lawsuit, a plumbing problem).

Don't write anything in your journal until later, and only if you want to. Instead, simply savor the moment and the day ahead. Don't focus on tomorrow or next week. Don't spend any time on the future. If something comes to mind you need to remember or do, jot it down quickly but don't think further of it. You'll have time for that. For now, just BE.

Fully there, fully observant.

Be, and be in the present.

> *"Don't worry about anything; instead, pray about everything. Tell God what you need and thank him for all he has done. Then you will experience God's peace, which*

exceeds anything we can understand. His peace will guard your hearts and minds as you live in Christ Jesus." Philippians 4:6-9

"Many people say, 'Who will show us better times?' Let your face shine on us, Lord. You have given me greater joy than those who have abundant harvests of grain and new wine. In peace I will lie down and sleep, for you alone, O Lord, will keep me safe." Psalm 4:6-8

Key Thought: The present is a gift. Live it fully, and you'll improve the future at the same time.

Habit Five:

The Habit of Specific Thinking

Day Seventeen

Specific vs Global Thinking

The next good habit is one I'll call specific thinking. Since it's far easier to describe its opposite, global thinking, we'll start there. What is global thinking? It is the tendency to see life in big unchanging categories instead of smaller bits. Much of life is composed of small events, some good, some bad, and a lot of neutral. A few bad bits don't make everything bad. When someone thinks globally, he or she is likely to label something as *bad*, instead of looking at all the component parts to find the shades that *aren't* so bad.

Let's take an example. If you wake up and it's raining, you spill coffee on your outfit, and then miss your bus, you might label it a "bad" day, even before it gets started. If you identify it that way early on, it's likely that you'll be convinced all day that it's a "bad" day. You'll tell your colleagues, spouse, or others how bad your day was. Talking about it, of course, will make you feel even worse about it. This is an example of global thinking, globally taking the whole day as bad, when in fact, only a couple of events were unfortunate or inconvenient. The rest of the day may have been productive and even pleasant.

In the 1960s, a psychologist named Aaron Beck noticed that some of his patients had patterns in their way of viewing the world that were counterproductive. He called these patterns cognitive distortions. You could even call them bad mental habits or filters. A cognitive distortion is a tendency in our thinking that distorts or deforms events or facts. One cognitive distortion that has been identified is called a mental filter, and it's like global thinking. It expands on the negative aspect of something or someone and overlooks anything positive. It is a common, though unfortunate, habit that leads to pessimism and snap judgments. Is everything in a given situation *really* negative? If you had to, you could probably pull out something positive about it. And if you make that practice a habit, hardly anything will be purely negative.

Global Habits Up Close

Bring to mind a person you know who you consider selfish or disagreeable. Acknowledge that this person has many aspects. He can be unpleasant when under stress, but when he is relaxed, he's generous and fun. This way of responding to a person you find difficult will help you be more patient with him when he's stressed-out, and more appreciative of the positive traits he has at other times.

People often think globally with bosses, leaders, or politicians they don't like— *everything* is bad about this person, and *nothing* is good. If he or she makes a decision or passes a bill you approve of, it was still done for selfish reasons. For you, that person can never win. That's an example of global thinking. Agreeing with certain things and disagreeing with others would be more fair-minded. If that person is someone in authority, you may simply be afraid of what he or she will do that might affect you negatively. This could also apply to someone you don't know well, but for some reason, dislike. Maybe you've seen them in a limited situation that didn't turn out so well. You may see only a small part of who they really are, instead of assuming they have many different aspects to their personality.

We might do the same thing with pieces of information that we hear second-hand. Even news from a reputable source can be slanted a particular way. In fact, there is very little information available anywhere that is entirely reliable and fully neutral. We may develop fears or strong opinions based on untrustworthy information. Ask yourself, is this true? Am I sure? What was the source? Where did he or she hear it? Beware of the phrase "I heard that . . ." This phrase may supply completely unfounded rumors you may then take as fact and end up letting it affect your thoughts and emotions. Practice more objectivity, more distance when you hear something, and be sure to evaluate it critically. Don't believe everything you hear, without reflection. Pursue the facts and, as much as possible, base your thoughts and attitudes on them.

Global thinking also forms convictions very quickly with little information, the famous "knee-jerk" reaction. A person forming this kind of evaluation will often defend it with much emotion and hostility, even though there is little backing it up in knowledge or in life experience. Sometimes we form iron-strong opinions based on what we heard from someone we like. Learn to question sources, even other Christians. No one is infallible, and the other person may have gotten incomplete information as well. That doesn't show disrespect to the person who gave you the information. It shows respect to *your* thought process and your need to have facts available before forming an opinion, or at least to recognize that there must be more to the story than what you have heard.

Tomorrow, we'll see how to develop or improve specific thinking.

Steps for the Journey

As you read the section for today, did you identify any patterns of thinking in yourself? Do you tend to specific or global thinking?

Write down some examples of each one from your life. If no instances of specific thinking come to mind, maybe it's an area you need to improve.

Global thinking examples:

Specific thinking examples:

List any negative outcomes for you or others of having a global outlook.

Take a sweeping survey of your life. Do you consider it to have one overriding quality, such as good, bad, boring, or difficult? Identify the word you use most often. Then underneath that word, write five *other* words (not synonyms of the first one) to add different aspects to the description of your life.

Write a list of up to 5 things you consider to be wrong in your life. Then write at least 10 things in your life that are good and you're thankful for—positive, pleasant, or promising. Look at both lists. Can you see that your life is made up of both positive and what you perceive as negative? Every life has both. This helps to normalize the negative, putting it back into perspective. Maybe you'll see that the good things hold more weight than the bad things, which tend to be more temporary.

What's Wrong?
1.
2.
3.
4.

5.

What's Right?
1
2.
3.
4.
5.
6.
7.
8.
9.
10.

Think of 3 situations that have happened or could happen to someone, real or hypothetical, that are *worse* than yours. Write them down. Consider each one in detail. Live in it mentally for a moment, as if it is happening to you. Now review your situation. Does it feel less "bad"? Less dramatic?

1.

2.

3.

List several situations, attitudes, issues and/or people in your life that you don't like and feel negatively about. Write one phrase about why you don't like them. Then mentally break each one into parts, both positive and negative. Write at least two positives for each one. Look at your list of both negative and positive aspects of the person or situation. Doesn't that change your feelings? Can you honestly admit that some positive or potentially positive aspects exist in that person or situation?

1.

2.

3.

When you catch yourself thinking globally about a situation, stop and jot some notes in your journal or in the space below. Be honest with yourself. Compare your habits with the plumbline of Scripture. How does God want you to react to each of these global attitudes?

Break that situation down into several parts, making sure that you include some good things in the list. Look over the list and begin to develop the habit of seeing life as a collection of specific things, not a global mass of badness. Record how this makes you think or feel differently than before.

Day Eighteen

Critical or Emotional Thinking?

Critical thinking (which has nothing to do with criticizing but seeks to look objectively at all sides) is flagrantly absent in our society. The popular vote of the group determines the truth. What's almost universally agreed upon seems to be right. But is it? Aren't there usually more sides to a story than that? Are we swept on a wave of hysteria or common conviction that we haven't fully investigated or thought through for ourselves?

We owe it to ourselves to take the time to ask what *we* think of something and (importantly) what backs up our belief, to think *specifically* instead of globally, and to own our thoughts and opinions.

In our day, it seems more evident than ever that the view of the largest majority influences what is considered correct thinking, rather than allowing for differences. Those who diverge from the popular narrative may be criticized or otherwise silenced. This response is dangerous and erodes our individual right to think and decide issues for ourselves, based on our faith and our convictions.

Let's take critical thinking to a personal level. In your life, you may look at certain factors and conclude that *everything* is going wrong, and your life is a total mess. Stop and ask yourself, is it true? Is *everything* going wrong? That is global thinking. Ask instead, what things are going right? Remember the parts—some parts might not be so good, but other parts are. Maybe you've had one or two romantic flops in your recent past. Does that mean you'll *never* have a good relationship again? Of course not.

Much of global thinking is black and white thinking. It is dramatic, swinging our emotions from one end of the spectrum to the other. Some people are addicted to drama. This brings excitement into their lives, though they likely don't recognize this (and if they were honest, they don't really like it). It might be more boring to see things in their true, multifaceted perspective, but it will give you more peace if you accept the grays and don't look for drama.

Do you tend to think first with your emotions? Emotions aren't completely unreliable. Listening to our "gut" can provide valuable input, as we calmly tune into our perception *and* the facts that we have available. This is very different from an impulsive emotional reaction which hasn't taken time to carefully include the facts.

Conviction vs. Judgment

Among some Christians, global thinking mixes with religious conviction and the result can only be called judgmental or closed-minded. Nonbelievers sometimes claim that Christians are judgmental and, unfortunately, some of them are. Striving toward a godly lifestyle is essential in the Christian life, but if it causes us to measure others against *our* standard, or categorize without reflection, we begin to violate the love that Jesus showed to all kinds of people. Of course, it is important to have convictions. But they should not cause us to come to a quick judgment before knowing all the facts. Sometimes the criticism is the worst among believers or Christian groups. We assume every Christian *ought* to have the same convictions as we do about everything. No wonder the world watches in wonder as we tear each other down.

Of all people, we should demonstrate the same love and nonjudgmental openness that Jesus showed without distinction. Followers of Jesus should be capable of separating the weak threads of a person's character from the strong, positive ones. We affirm the strong side, instead of only judging the weakness. Doing this will make us more patient, accepting, and much more like Christ. The importance of showing love was one of the final mandates Jesus gave before He went to the cross. That's how important those words are to us today. The beautiful result of practicing specific thinking is extending *grace*—the shining distinction of Christianity.

Another bad habit we might develop after numerous years in the church is accepting non-critically everything we hear, as we fall into group thinking. Even though most practicing Christians believe the same major Biblical doctrines, in matters of daily life and extra-biblical opinions, there should be diversity and reflection and freedom to be different. Many Christians lose their ability to think, because of mindlessly following everything the church group says or believes. We are often too influenced by our church peers to think and speak up for ourselves, or even form our own opinions about something.

If we're not careful, thinking will become a lost art. Specific thinking helps us maintain our individuality in how we approach life, even as believers. We may have similar doctrinal beliefs, but we shouldn't all hold the same opinions about everything else. That would be too boring! Can we have unity *and* diversity even in the family of God? Yes, and we should!

Multicolored Thinking

In summary, the habit of specific thinking breaks every person and situation into parts, acknowledging that little in life is all black or white. There are many colors and grays. This helps us be more patient with differences. As you consider yourself, you know that you aren't all bad or all good, but a mixture. The same is true with other people and situations.

You'll be able to recognize that some parts of your day or life situation are fine, even if others aren't so much. Then there are the dull pieces, and that's okay. We wouldn't want to live in a roller coaster of drama and excitement all the time as if we were starring in a thriller movie!

We can live in the moment and take individual events less seriously. And this can significantly lower our blood pressure. As you develop this habit, it will be rare for you to have a bad day, because you will no longer label the whole thing as "bad" if just one negative event occurs. You'll recognize that, though one negative event may have happened, the rest of the day was either neutral or positive. With practice, you can identify something worthwhile, even if it was just the absence of a headache or fatigue you had the day before. Yes, bad days do come along, but not nearly as often as we may think.

As specific thinking becomes a habit, that is, seeing life and people in their component parts instead of good or bad, you'll probably end up using the words "good" and "bad" less and less. You'll develop a broader vocabulary, richer and more multi-colored, than the black and white language of global thinking.

Steps for the Journey

If you haven't done this already, evaluate each day for several days. Identify the high points and, if you have any, the low points. You may be surprised to see fewer low points than you thought. And they may strike you as minor compared to the high points. Record any notes here that you find from this reflection.

What changes would you like to make to encourage specific thinking in yourself?

How does this habit tie into the habit of positive thinking?

How does this habit tie into the habit of interpretations?

As a Christian, do you sometimes judge others who aren't like you?

Do you ever fall into black and white thinking (i.e., everything Christian is white and everything else is black, or to be avoided)? Be honest. Jot down typical situations where this occurs.

Do the people you most often spend time with encourage divergent opinions, critical thinking, or expressions of your unique personality? Do they prefer that you agree with them? Or do you prefer that they agree with you?

How likely are you to accept what another believer has said without reflecting on whether it's even true? (They might be misinformed, jumping to conclusions, or exaggerating, for example.)

How do process information you receive? For example, news from a political or news program, a bit of gossip about a friend or family member, information from an article, website, or other source. Do you usually form an opinion quickly based on what you've heard, or are you more likely to see both sides of an issue? Test yourself for the next couple of days to see what your reflexes are.

Try the following experiment for several days. Carry around a small notepad or something else on which you can jot notes easily. Be aware of situations where you are receiving information throughout the day. Some possible sources: Morning news, editorial program on the radio, coffee pot conversations with colleagues or after church, any expression of opinions or opinions *disguised as facts* (be careful about this one) coming from friends, family, or colleagues. If possible, stop for two to three minutes to jot down the situation and reflect on what else could be going on aside from what was presented. Practice this famous advice: Don't believe everything you hear. Your notebook will be full of interesting versions of news by the end of a week.

If you have difficulty thinking critically about a news program you watch regularly, refrain from watching or listening to the program for one or two weeks. Then pretend you are someone who has no background on the program and listen to it with a more neutral stance. What do you observe?

Once in a while, try to mentally step outside of the context you're in and look down on it as objectively as possible. What do you observe?

As believers, we're told we have the mind of Christ. How does this apply to the habit of specific thinking?

"Always be humble and gentle. Be patient with each other, making allowance for each other's faults because of your love." Ephesians 4:2

"The Lord directs the steps of the godly. He delights in every detail of their lives. Though they stumble, they will never fall, for the Lord holds them by the hand." Psalm 37:23-24

Key Thought: Look at life in its separate parts, and gain a wiser, happier perspective.

Habit Six

The Habit of Self-Responsibility

Day Nineteen

Agents or Victims?

When you hear the word "responsibility" do you automatically envision doing homework, taking out the garbage, or paying child support? Does this word cause you to square your shoulders and mutter, "Oh, alright, then," as you grudgingly agree to do your duty? That is only one tiny part of taking responsibility, and it isn't the focus of this chapter. You can breathe a sigh of relief now.

This mental habit will set you free to be the agent in your life instead of a victim. In fact, the best news (and an important assumption in this entire book) is that you are *not* a victim. You can act in your world and in the daily details of your life. You can make changes in your life, and you can make a difference in the lives of others. That is the core of the habit of self-responsibility. It may include doing homework or working at a particular job as part of a larger goal, but it is more life-changing and revolutionary than we've ever dared believe.

Let's stop for a moment and address the question that is likely in your mind. What about God? If we believe He is our Lord and our lives are in His hands, how does this balance with *our* initiative in our lives? This is a common question. As soon as we become Christians, we realize that our lives are in God's hands. It's tempting to assume we don't have any responsibility for the direction of our lives. It's all up to Him. Is this what's meant by trusting God, becoming passive in our lives? This may be closer to fatalism than Christianity.

A Gift from God

Every human being has a *will*, including desires and hopes. God gave us a will for a reason. Obeying Him in love is one reason but taking action in our lives for our own good and the good of other people is another. He never intended for us to float along through our lives, hoping for His intervention at every turn. If we do our part and let God do His, and we don't violate His revealed will, there should be a good balance between our will, expressed in our decisions and actions, and God's.

The problem is, we don't always know the balance. We hear "wait on the Lord," which is appropriate advice when we are hoping for an answer to prayer to something that we have no control over (once we have done our part.) It isn't an appropriate response if we are neglecting something important that *we* are supposed to do. Taking responsibility appropriately is necessary for a godly lifestyle, as well as a happy life, as many Christian books on the market assert.

It isn't wrong to set goals or pursue objectives that we want, unless we have a goal that clearly violates God's Word. Rather, setting goals and trying to achieve them is a wise practice to help us have the lives we desire. And our desires are a healthy expression of our uniqueness. Human will empowers responsible action in our lives, the lives God has entrusted to us. Yes, we are entrusted to Him too, since He is our heavenly Father, but the life He gives us, He expects us to live responsibly with our strength and mind as well as guidance from His Word and His Spirit who indwells us. This doesn't exclude godly counsel from other believers, if it's needed, for a goal such as starting a business or moving to a new city.

Responsibility Breakdown

A man we'll call Joe is lonely. He believes the people in his neighborhood and his workplace are unfriendly snobs. He goes home after work every day to an empty apartment and watches television until he goes to bed. In discussing the problem with his brother, Frank, Frank suggests that Joe join a club, start attending church, or take a class in order to meet people. But Joe has ready reasons why he can't do any of the things Frank suggests. Frank asks Joe to consider how he behaves around other people, to determine if he has any annoying habits that might be turning other people off. Frank asks Joe to consider how he can become more likeable and approachable. Joe insists that his colleagues and neighbors are simply unfriendly jerks. Joe isn't a victim, but he firmly believes he is. Joe will be lonely for a *long* time.

How often do we look at a problem and immediately assume its cause as well as the solution are outside of us? Doing this shuts the door to an answer before we even begin. It leaves the solution "out there," and so we wait as helpless victims to be rescued. The helpless victim is usually disgruntled and unhappy (and probably complains a lot). Wouldn't it be far better to ask, "What can I do about this?" and attempt to find a solution?

Certain people take responsibility for everyone they know except themselves. They try to make others happy but ignore their own needs. They try to influence others to make certain decisions in their lives but bypass their own backlog of tasks. This is backward and leads to unhappiness and frustration for all parties. You can only take responsibility for the life that is *yours*.

Sometimes in the church we believe we need to do whatever people ask of us to be good Christians, while ignoring our own needs and gifts. This is not what God asks of us in order to please Him. You'll see that clearly in the Scriptures that speak of spiritual gifting. Gifts are different for a reason: We're *not* necessarily supposed to do whatever is needed. (Although giving a hand in a temporary task where there's a need is a positive way to contribute and help.) Trying to please others all the time will wear you out and leave you resentful. And pleasing others shouldn't be our goal, anyway. Doing what *we* want to do and what we're gifted to do doesn't always occur to us, even though *our desire or lack of desire is often an inner signal that the Holy Spirit uses to guide us.*

One consequence of victim thinking and passivity is depression. If we feel powerless, we feel trapped and hopeless. Hopelessness leads to depression and lethargy. That's because your hope lies beyond your ability, as you wait for the dramatic rescue from the outside. Psychologists call this the "locus of control," which refers to where your sense of control comes from, inside or outside of you. They confirm a link between powerlessness and depression. Yet, as soon as you *decide* to do something about your situation, as soon as you realize you *can* act, you feel better, often in a matter of minutes.

Here is a harsh reality that may surprise you: In most cases, you created your current life, whether you know it or not. It is your masterpiece, even if you despise it. If you go back in time, in many cases, you'll see how you participated in the circumstances that led you to where you are today. True, some things happen to us, but our response can change our life experience afterward, whether salvaging something positive from the unfortunate incident, or sealing its sad consequences into our lives. In Dr. Phil McGraw's book, *Life Strategies*, he emphasizes the importance of acknowledging and accepting our role in creating the results of our lives. He says we can learn to make better choices so that we'll have better lives. This means you *can* have better, if you own up to your responsibility and decide to make changes. The word "decide" is a magic key, followed by "do".

Steps for the Journey

What are your initial thoughts after reading this chapter? Do you agree, disagree?

Consider your way of thinking about your life. Do you lean more on the victim side or the agent side? Do you tend to let solutions come from outside or to let problems persist for a long time before acting? Or do you tend to take action quickly?

How do you think God interacts with human will? What does He expect of you in solving your problems or pursuing your goals?

What changes do you need to make in this habit?

What are some areas of your life where you'd like to be more of an agent than a victim?

Identifying these will be a start to a positive process. What results do you want from the area you identified? Isn't that a great reason to be proactive and take responsibility?

List two things you'll do first for that area.

Day Twenty

More Powerful Than You Think

Accepting responsibility isn't popular. Blaming others seems more convenient and less painful, whether we are blaming our parents, the government, our spouse, or our boss. There is a big problem with this, however. It may be comfortable, but it keeps you in prison. Dr. David Viscott speaks to this in his book, *Finding Your Strength in Difficult Times,* stating that the most significant obstacles in attaining the life we want are within us. Sometimes we don't want to let these obstacles go, even if they are uncomfortable, because they provide safety from risk. We need to be willing to give up the security of those blockages in order to move forward. C. S. Lewis was on the same wavelength when he said, "The door to hell is locked from the inside."*

It is all too easy for us to remain passive and fearful under the guise of "waiting for God" and "bearing up patiently" in a situation that maybe we can and should change ourselves. Pray for strength and a good outcome . . . then develop a strategy of change. We might wonder if a course of action is God's will before we will move forward, and we shouldn't neglect committing it to him. Many decisions are neutral. Should you become a doctor or a novelist? Of course, you'll want God's guidance. Pray for this decision, do your research, evaluate your aptitudes and desires, as well as the opportunities, unless God has clearly shown you otherwise. The domain of God's will for your life is broader than you may think. "Commit everything you do to the Lord, trust him, and he will help you." Psalm 37:5

With this mental habit, we assume that *we* are responsible for our lives and its consequences. We don't blame other people for what goes wrong or what is inconvenient. We own up to our part of a problem if it applies. And we understand that there is a lot we *can* do to not only fulfill our responsibilities but change things for the better and pursue our dreams.

This puts empowerment solidly back into our hands, and that's excellent news. Why? Because we can do something instead of just suffering and waiting through whatever happens to us. We can correct mistakes we have made in the past; we can plan for a better tomorrow. Yes, it's more work. Many people would rather whine about things, sometimes repeatedly, than take action. But acting leads to better outcomes.

You have only one life. Don't let it drift randomly along and find yourself ten years from now in roughly the same place you are right now, with the same discontents, the same weaknesses, and the same lack of opportunities.

Self-Responsibility Defined

There are two aspects of this mental habit. First, it means living with an assumption that we are responsible for our actions and their consequences. We are responsible for *ourselves*. Even if things happen to us that we didn't choose, we are responsible for our response. This is empowering, because we always have this choice and it will make our lives better, whatever we are experiencing.

Melodie Beattie points out in her book, *Codependent No More*, that we are responsible for our physical, spiritual, emotional, and financial well-being, for trying to solve our own problems or live with the ones we can't solve. We are responsible for our own goals, and for what we give and receive from people. Our happiness is our responsibility, no one else's. If we take responsibility for each of these areas of our lives, we won't have any need to blame others or try to extract our satisfaction from other people.

The second aspect of the habit of self-responsibility is a tendency toward action, toward solving problems, taking initiative for what you want. This is one of the main characteristics of leaders, seeing a challenge and not assuming it's someone else's job to figure it out. The result of this habit is that you'll have more control over the desired outcomes of your life. This isn't a matter of trying to control everything and everyone around you but taking responsibility instead of leaving things passively to neglect, or to someone else. We often give other people the responsibility of our happiness: a partner, a child, a parent, a friend, a boss, or God. We are setting ourselves up for disappointment because other people can't assure our happiness. Only we can. We know ourselves best. No one will take responsibility for us. And even God won't do for us what we should do for ourselves.

Steps for the Journey

In her book, *Codependent No More*, author Melodie Beattie asserts that we are responsible for our own happiness. Do you agree? Disagree?

Do you think that God wants this for you? (Hint: See John 10:10)

What are some ways you can improve your level of contentment with your life?

In the same book, Beattie states that we are responsible for our physical, spiritual, emotional, and financial well-being. In which of these areas do you need to take more initiative, more self-responsibility? Apply this not only to problems but also goals you may have.

Consider the following passages as they relate to your action balanced with God's sovereign will for your life.

Psalm 37:3-6

Proverbs 3:5-6

Commit your goals to God in prayer. He will give you the strength and wisdom to follow-through.

Day Twenty-One

Make Your Life Better

As we move forward, there will be obstacles that rise up on our path, such as self-doubt, fear of rejection, laziness, or fear of consequences (or even fear of success). There will also be external barriers. Problems that distract your attention, friends or loved ones who don't support your goal or understand the benefits of taking responsibility for your life. They may disagree with your decisions or even with the effort involved in changing your mental habits. Stay the course. They'll see the benefits, and if they don't, you surely will. This habit will move the needle in your life in the areas that are most important to you. Take small steps, despite the obstacles, and your confidence will grow. God has promised to guide you and strengthen you in the journey. (Psalm 32:8)

This proactive tendency is the opposite of passivity. Passivity is certainly easier but holds a dark danger: Life passes you by. Years go by without growth, without fulfillment, seeing the same weaknesses cycle back around. Bitterness festers as we blame others instead of acting. Opportunities are lost, and we don't accomplish our dreams. A sad story of a passive, but not very unusual, life.

You have the ability (and supernatural help) to make your life better, whether you want to resolve a problem or accomplish a treasured goal. An awareness of your needs and your desires is the first step, followed by the commitment to put your capacities, energy, intelligence, and will to work on it. Identify your barriers, whether low self-esteem, laziness, lack of information or training or fear of others' opinions (among other fears). Sometimes we make a goal but are unmotivated because we don't want it enough. Maybe we'll need to discover why, or else change that goal, choosing one that excites us and makes us feel alive.

God gives us gifts and abilities and equips us for specific tasks. He promises to empower us with his strength and guide us with his wisdom. He wants us to live daily dependent on these resources from Him, not just in ministry, but in every area of life. He lives through us if we yield to Him moment by moment. That's the best equipping you could ask for! (John 15:5)

What you do in this life counts. It has often been said that life is not a dress rehearsal. What you do, not what you intend or talk about, will make the difference. Passivity begets more passivity, but once in motion, it's far easier to continue to move. If you develop a habit that empowers you to make a difference instead of following the majority, who simply complain about it, it will revolutionize your life, as well as the progress of your future dreams.

Steps for the Journey

Make a list of at least four situations that frustrate you. Under each item, list at least two things you can do about that situation.

Here's an example: Problem: My neighbor makes noise and disturbs my sleep every weekend. What I can do: 1) talk to him, 2) after talking to him, go to police. Second example: I need new software for my business but don't know what to get. What I can do: 1) Do research online, 2) ask knowledgeable friends, 3) ask at an office-supply store what they recommend, 4) ask someone who does the same work that you do what kind of software they use and how they like it. Choose one or more of these options until you make your decision.

If you break down the steps, they don't seem too overwhelming.

Your turn:

Problem:

What I can do:
1)

2)

Problem:

What I can do:

1)

2)

Problem:

What I can do:
1)

2)

Write down one or two circumstances you don't like as well as ways in which YOU created or contributed to the problems. Be honest and don't skip this part. Then write one or two (at least) plans for what you will do about this.

Situation:

My part:

What I can now do:

Situation:

My part:

What I can now do:

Journal a few sentences recording your response to this section on self-responsibility.

Day Twenty-Two

Decide to Decide (Trust is a Choice)

Reflecting on self-responsibility seems at first like a burden, until you realize how freeing it is. To escape from a victim, powerless, or passive mentality is exhilarating, especially the moment you understand that you can *do* something about a problem you may have just tolerated up to now, or a dream you want to pursue.

One barrier to taking responsibility for certain parts of our lives might be a deficit in faith. We have faith for general areas of our lives and for our eternal home with God, but do we believe He'll empower and lead us as we go out on a brand-new limb? We call this "stepping out in faith" for a reason. Surely, the Israelites were fearful and hesitant as they huddled on the threshold of the Promised Land, knowing there were enemies there they'd have to conquer. God instructed the people and Joshua to not be afraid since He Himself planned to take down their opponents and lead them to victory.

Many times in Scripture, we're told to have faith, trust God, or not be afraid. If it's a command in God's Word, it must be possible. We place our faith and trust in the One we know. If we have trouble trusting, we may need to get to know God better, both in His Word and by personal experience. Fear is an emotion, and the only control we have over our emotions is to change our thoughts. Trust is a *choice*. Yes, it's a command, too, but we choose to obey or not. And as we see throughout the Bible and throughout our lives, when we decide to obey and trust, the outcome is better, and our confidence in God is strengthened. Which makes it easier to trust the next time, as our trust muscles are developed!

Pursue Your Dreams

You can also do something about your dreams and the direction of your life. Consider your dreams. What are they? A new career? A dream vacation? Writing a book? Having a new home? Creating or participating in a particular ministry or reaching out to someone or a group of people? Or you may even want to completely redesign your life.

Write down some long-term desires you have for yourself. (It's okay if they're really big and you think they're unrealistic. You're just dreaming at this point.)

1.

2.

3.

4.

Start now thinking about smaller steps you can do already that'll help you to achieve your dreams. Make your list of the dreams or goals, then for each item, make a secondary list of smaller steps (getting information, getting training, networking with people) you would have to do beforehand in order to accomplish them. Suddenly, the dream seems more realistic and achievable. Pray and commit this dream and the process to God (Psalm 37:5), asking for His leading and will. Then get moving! He will help you!

Write some of your steps here:
Goal:

Steps:

Goal:

Steps:

Goal:

Steps:

What obstacles do you need to consider? (Finances, lack of training, support of family members, the need to network with people). What will you do to move these obstacles out of your way?

How will your life look once some of these goals are accomplished? Consider one at a time.

Commit them to God and His will. Ask Him for wisdom and direction. He promises He will give it!

Read Ephesians 2:10. What does it say about you and how God equips you?

What might be some "good things" He has in mind for you to do, according to the way He's gifted you? (Spiritual *and* natural gifts)

In Day 16, you read a list of encouraging passages about how our God guides us throughout our lives. Here is that list again to soak in God's promises of guidance (plus a few more). If you didn't read and meditate on these passages yet (or even if you did), take time to do it now.

Isaiah 48:17

Psalm 138:8

Jeremiah 29:11

Psalm 139:16

Psalm 32:8

Psalm 16:7-8

John 10:27

Isaiah 30:21

And also:

Psalm 25: 4-5, 10

Psalm 37:23-4

Psalm 18:32-36

We commit our ways to Him, but we trust Him to guide us along the way, even as we exercise our will and self-responsibility.

Record your observations of any different feelings or attitudes you notice once you've begun to develop a mental habit of self-responsibility.

"The Lord says, 'I will guide you along the best pathway for your life. I will advise you and watch over you.'" Psalm 32:8

Key Thought: God has His role in your life, and He gives you YOURS. Make the most of it!

Habit Seven

The Habit of Openness

Day Twenty-Three

Open vs. Closed

Are you ready to widen the borders of your usual thought patterns? This will add enjoyment to every area of your life. New facts, places, and people will add zest to an otherwise predictable, uninspired mental palate. This isn't a travel ad, but a foretaste of the next habit.

What is this habit about?

You've probably met people who practice the habit of openness. They come to a new situation anticipating that they will learn or gain something, meet someone interesting, or enjoy their day. These people are receptive from the start, not blocking themselves off from anything new before they find out what's there.

When we meet such people, we like being around them. They are multifaceted and are able to discuss many things. They show interest in other people, even those who are very different from themselves. They are good listeners, not deciding quickly or judging before hearing or interrupting so they can state their opinion right away. They respond honestly after evaluating, instead of saying what they think you want to hear or reacting according to their pre-programmed ideas. They are approachable. They don't have a preset agenda. And their self-worth doesn't ride on whether or not you agree with them. They are simply comfortable with who they are but are willing to leave themselves aside for a moment in order to hear what *you* think. These people are rare and refreshing.

The Hazards of the Closed Mind

It is easier to see this habit in light of its contrast, the closed mind. Having a closed mind blocks us from much of what life has to offer. We spend our years experiencing only a tiny percentage of all the things we could be enjoying, simply because we are closed to them or may not even know they are there. You might not wish to sample an area completely opposed to your Christian beliefs, but there are many neutral subjects, activities, and places to learn about, if you'll take the time and get a little bit curious.

A closed mind seals out helpful solutions to a problem that a person may have, ones that could save him or her from disaster or inconvenience. A closed mind also blocks creativity. The closed mind turns away from opportunities or facts that could enable the accomplishment of dreams and life-long objectives, or the discovery of a fun new activity. Let's face it, we don't know everything about everything. We haven't reached our full capacity as human beings. Many researchers say that most of us function at only 10% of our mental capacity and potential. Being open enables us to get smarter, more effective, more successful, and happier.

A closed-minded person doesn't put himself or herself into question, and this damages relationships and sabotages opportunities. You've likely heard about the smart, talented man or woman whose lack of social skills and hot temper lost the contract or the job or the marriage. We need emotional openness too, not only to get along with others, but because it smooths the path toward achieving our objectives. One of the top traits that many companies value in their managers is good interpersonal skills, many of which begin with openness toward others.

Relationship Gold

Speaking of relationships, problems in this area are among the most painful and frequent complications of our lives, yet we don't often seek ways to prevent them. Being more open with others can soften or prevent conflicts. It improves the quality of our relationships and allow us to be more pleasant company. One tip is to *not* assume your way is the right one. The other person has a valid opinion too.

We need to be courageous enough to ask questions like these: Could I have done this differently? Did I say something to offend her? Should I have been more patient? Did I assume the answer instead of finding out? Did I act arrogant? Could I have been gentler in that interaction? They are also able to say, "I'm sorry. I shouldn't have spoken that way. I'll try harder. I'll try something different." This is relational openness. Learning to relate to others in this way demonstrates patience, love, and gentleness . . . the fruit of the Spirit. (Galatians 5:22-23)

In a conversation, ask questions and let the other person talk, too. Show interest. Try to really understand what he is saying and give him time to express himself. Summarize what you hear him saying, to make sure you've got it right. It will make him feel validated and respected that you listened and understood him so well.

Many times, we shut off other people due to lack of interest, subconsciously believing that what we have to say is more important. Can we pick up a subtle invitation another person might give us to ask them more, to go deeper? Do we need to improve our listening skills? If we practice this way of openness in relationships, people will enjoy being with us, and we'll enjoy *them* much more as well.

The part of our brain responsible for emotions (the amygdala) reacts much faster than the part which handles rational thinking (neocortex). Our emotional mind is also often fueled by childhood patterns and hurts from the past. The emotional mind isn't always reliable yet may drive a lot of our closed thinking. We owe it to ourselves to develop a habit of slowing down our knee-jerk reactions, whether they are emotions, opinions, or both, giving room for reason and understanding.

Steps for the Journey

How open are you? Rate yourself honestly in your journal or the space below.

Here are some questions to help you dig deeper into your activity patterns. Write your responses or just reflect on them.

- In the evening I usually: (e.g. watch TV, read, other, talk on the phone, work on the computer).

- On the weekend I usually:

- How often do I do things that are different?

- What books have I read in the last 6 months? How often do I read or go online in order to learn something new?

- What subjects do I read about? Are they the same ones all within one genre, or a variety?

- What activities do I do regularly? How likely (on a scale of 1-5) am I to try something new? (5 being very likely) How often in a given year do I try something really different? (never, often, occasionally, rarely, never)

- What people do I spend the most time with? How different are my friends from me, culturally, racially, in personality, in social status?

- How often do I meet new people? How different are they from me?

- How do I usually respond when I meet someone who is different from me or whose values are different from mine?

- Do most of my friends think exactly like I do on most issues?

- When I hear new information, have I usually made up my mind beforehand?

- How much am I influenced by tradition, culture, religion, family, or habits?

- How likely am I to listen to someone and give them a fair hearing before making up my mind?

- Do I listen to someone attentively, or do I have the habit of interrupting him or her with my own ideas? Has anyone ever told me that I have this habit of interrupting?

What are my conclusions after answering these questions? Do I need to open up a little more? How?

This is just a start to our reflection on openness, but hopefully it has gotten you interested in exploring this area in greater depth in coming days.

Day Twenty-Four

Be Curious. Be a Bridge

Some people aren't curious about anything outside of their daily habits and knowledge. Others are afraid of exposure to anything that doesn't exactly match their experiences or their family, traditional, or religious beliefs. They fear that exposure to something—anything—different will weaken or insult their beliefs or traditions.

It doesn't have to, if they approach these things with objective curiosity, as if they are learning a subject in school. There's no need to feel personally threatened or uncomfortable. It's just information. You decide how you wish to use it.

Being closed-minded is like being inside an airtight capsule, allowing little entrance of new information or new influences. Sadly, this describes many people in the church. They aren't interested in anything that doesn't come from a Christian source or assume that there is nothing of value there for them. They may end up missing out on a lot of interesting and helpful information that in no way compromises their beliefs. If their convictions are solidly anchored in their lives, any diverse viewpoints they encounter through relationships, books, movies, or experiences shouldn't rock their boat of faith, but rather enlarge their perspective and even strengthen their beliefs.

At the same time, some believers blindly accept anything coming from someone who claims to be a Christian. We know from how many denominations and cults exist that there are many ways people interpret doctrine. Other Christians can make mistakes, push their viewpoint, or say things we don't agree with. We have as much need to think critically when reading Christian books or listening to a sermon as we do when hearing the news or reading a magazine. We can and should exercise critical thinking *whatever* we encounter and not allow the pastor, the church, or our Christian friends to do our thinking for us. It would be a shame to ignore or reject the wonderful gift we have of evaluating and thinking. The plumbline we go back to in each case is Scripture.

Differences in Opinion

We may find ourselves with people who are different from us, sometimes *very* different. We may find we have nothing to say to them, or we're uncomfortable or even feel threatened. A bit of curiosity helps! Ask a question to break the ice. Maybe we haven't exposed ourselves to anything new in a long time and have become limited. We are in a mental rut, and we get bored. *And* we become boring. Be curious. Ask questions. Be willing to learn from someone else.

Accepting another person as he or she is doesn't mean you necessarily approve or agree with their lifestyle. It's more a matter of validating their right to live the way they want, and their value as human beings, despite differences. And it shows the love of Christ, who hung around people with *very* different values, but loved them anyway.

As Christians, we are called to be bridges to a world that needs Christ. This may begin by accepting the truth that out of more than seven billion people on the earth, there will be many individual lifestyles, personalities, and viewpoints. As we embrace this fact, and even delight in the colorful diversity of it, this will take us a long way toward the habit of openness. That doesn't mean you choose just anyone to be your friends or condone every possible lifestyle, but it does mean you accept people, as a general rule, the way they are, respecting their individuality.

When we encounter differences in opinion, we have an opportunity to demonstrate godly love through openness. Though we say we all have the right to our opinion, we may become uncomfortable or even feel threatened when someone disagrees with us, as if our views are being put down. This is probably not the case at all. We all need to slow down our frustration and remind ourselves we're only hearing opinions. We have ours. Others have theirs. There's no reason to be frustrated.

Often this comes to light when we are exposed to other cultures. Americans enjoy sharing the same viewpoint with their friends and are sometimes uncomfortable when faced with differing opinions. This may have its origins in the early history of the United States when many types of people had to get along together in the new land. By contrast, Europeans might disagree openly with each other (and in some countries, loudly with hand gestures), but they don't necessarily argue about it or stop speaking to one another. In their minds, differences make for interesting conversation. They don't become offended or hostile because someone doesn't agree with them. For the average French person, for example, when people always agree with each other, it's considered boring.

Keep Growing

Sometimes we stop growing, learning, and expanding after we leave school. We get into a routine, and we aren't curious anymore. We might be hesitant to learn new technologies, so we won't even try them, for fear of getting in over our heads. Unfortunately, people with this attitude also miss out on the practical side of technology. Once they're comfortable with it, the conveniences enable them to learn new things, keep in touch, and share their lives with others.

Many people don't improve or overcome their weaknesses for years, decades, or ever. That's a shame, for them, and the people who care about them. You have one life. Keep expanding that life. Keep growing and learning, all the way to the end.

Some of our life experiences are difficult and end up making us like a wall of concrete. We might carefully control what goes in and out to avoid further pain. A fresh hit from the outside in the form of a trial or an unexpected event knocks some stones out of that wall, and this can be a *gift in disguise*. That event can lead us to be more open and less self-protective, which will lead to a richer life. However, it's up to us if we let that event open us up or harden us even more.

Steps for the Journey

What are three areas you'd like to learn more about that you find interesting?

What will you do to begin learning about these?

Pick one to focus on in the coming week.

List some ways in the coming week that you can be more open in approaching new situations, learning new things, reading something you don't usually read, or experiencing something for the first time.

What are some new activities you would like to try (but have put off)? List them (at least three). When will you begin?

1.

2.

3.

From the following list, what category of person do you usually have a hard time relating to, getting along with, or accepting? For example, people who are different in

- Race
- Interests
- Appearance
- Age
- Socio economic status
- Level of hygiene
- Sexual preference
- Religious differences
- Moral choices
- Occupation
- Culture
- Political differences
- Other differences _____

What is a new way you can approach this person and think differently about him or her? How can you be more open about and toward this person, showing respect even if you don't share his/her opinion or lifestyle?

Be honest in answering the following questions:

- Do I sometimes get into arguments with people whose viewpoints are different from mine? (Theological, political, lifestyle, etc.)

- Am I more comfortable with people who are very much like me?

- Do I sometimes criticize people who are different from me, or have lifestyles that don't resemble mine?

- Do I have difficulty understanding how someone could like something that I don't like? Or dislike something that I like?

"Above all, clothe yourselves with love, which binds us all together in perfect harmony. And let the peace that comes from Christ rule in your hearts. Colossians 3:14-15a

Day Twenty-Five

A Big World

It's a big, interesting world. Imagine seeing it as a buffet table waiting to be sampled, as you choose. Here are more ideas to expand your life by being open.

- Make friends from other countries. You'll experience their view of things and learn about their customs and their homeland.

- Traveling will blow wide your worldview in unforgettable ways. You'll never be the same.

- Watch a documentary on a subject you know little about.

- Expose yourself to something out of your normal habit or comfort zone.

- Read a non-fiction book on a subject that interests you. Now with the prevalence of electronic readers and smart phones, you could carry multiple books with you very easily, for those spare moments waiting at a doctor's office or for a friend who is running late. Many people achieve their life objectives or overcome persistent life barriers by reading books.

- Learn to use the phrases "Why not?" and "I wonder why . . ." Develop curiosity, then follow up with lifestyle changes.

When I was a teenager sitting at the dinner table with a new dish in front of me, my stepfather would smile and say, "Don't try it, you might like it." Of course, his message was, if you try it, you may like it. But if you don't try it, you'll never know if you could have liked it. By trying something new, you may discover something enjoyable to add to your life.

The message is the same for each of us every day. DO try something. You may like it. Watch that program on traveling through India. You may never go to India, but you'll enjoy learning about it. DO sample dishes and meet people from other countries. DO read self-help, inner healing, or philosophy books that will challenge your thinking or help you work through a problem or a troublesome pattern in your life. *Be willing to grow and change.* Be ready to expand your thought processes and add to your subjects of interest.

Fresh Air

If you don't open up your mind to new information, it's like breathing your own air all the time. You do the same in your mind, recycling your ideas and habits, over and over. As you open the closed capsule of your thinking, many things will enter. Some you'll like, others you won't. Some you'll agree with, others you won't. This is the time to think critically. Not all information is right for you, and you have the intelligence to sift through it. But some of it is perfect for the place you are. Give it a try. It will add enrichment and enjoyment to your life and is a sure cure for boredom.

"If you need wisdom, ask our generous God, and he will give it to you. He will not rebuke you for asking." James 1:5

Steps for the Journey

Reread the paragraph about the person who is open (2nd full paragraph). How do you respond to this description? Would you like to be like this person? What would be the advantages for you? What would you have to change in your approach or outlook?

Record an honest evaluation of your level of openness. Would people describe you as an open person?

Are there any ways you've kept your life closed to certain areas because of fear or ignorance? If so, what are they? What are you afraid of? Is it legitimate, or not?

What are five steps you will take to become more open? (You can take some from the previous list if any of these piqued your interest.)

1.

2.

3.

4.

5.

"Sin is no longer your master, for you no longer live under the requirements of the law. Instead, you live under the freedom of God's grace." Romans 6:14

"This is what the Lord says—your Redeemer, the Holy One of Israel: 'I am the Lord your God, who teaches you what is good for you and leads you along the paths you should follow.'" Isaiah 48:17

Key Thought: Being more open will enrich your life and open your heart to love others better.

Habit Eight

Knowing Yourself

Day Twenty-Six

The Rudder of your Life

Knowing yourself is much more than a mental habit. It's a way of life, and it's the best way of life. That's a big statement, but you'll probably agree as you read this section. If you acquire all the other habits in the book but overlook this one, your life may be easier and you may be relatively content with it, but you will have missed the reason for which you are on the earth: to live YOUR life.

What is meant by "knowing yourself?" It includes understanding how you tick: knowing what you love, what you want, your likes, dislikes, your sense of humor, your personality, your weaknesses, and strengths . . . in short, your identity. It means that *you* are the reference point for your life, not others, whether in your decisions, outlook, or opinions. It doesn't imply focusing obsessively on yourself. It simply means knowing and following the real person you are, instead of a different person you may project to the world.

Knowing yourself doesn't push God out of the picture. On the contrary. He has made you as a unique individual with special likes, dislikes, gifts, and abilities. We saw in the chapter on self-esteem how much value God places on us as His special creations. He didn't make us as puppets. He made each one of us the manager, so to speak, of our lives. Your life is under your care and responsibility, no one else's. Your heart and God's Word together guide you daily. Making choices for your life according to the core *you,* will lead your life in the best way possible. But first, you need to *know* the core you.

Your Essential Self

In her book, *Finding Your Own North Star*, author Martha Beck speaks of something she calls your *essential self*. Your essential self, claims Beck, is the real you, as you were born, along with how you've developed through your early life. This includes your likes and dislikes, emotional reactions, quirks . . . your *real* personality. It is your identity, without the cultural or environmental trappings.

This is the core you. Your heart is your "navigational equipment", designed to take you to where you should be according to your true nature. In contrast, she explains that there is also the social self. The social self is based on what parents, society, and other people in your life think is good for you. Beck adds that, although the essential self is the real you, it should work in harmony with the social self.

In her book she gives examples of people who are out of touch with their essential, guiding selves. Too often, we live our lives strictly according to our social self and remain mostly clueless or deaf to our deeper essential self. The social self helps us attain what the essential self yearns for (such as connection, validation, and contribution), but too often we muffle its voice, either because we don't know what we truly want, or because we may be convinced that the consequences of disappointing the social self (and others) are too great.

The idea of two "selves"—an outward self-oriented toward other people, and an internal or real self—isn't new. As early as 1890, psychologist William James proposed three parts of the human being: the physical or material part, the social self, or identity perceived by others, and the spiritual self, or the inner core of identity. His "spiritual" self includes a person's goals and beliefs and may correspond to Beck's "essential self." Later theorists have expanded on the idea of a social self. In 1922 C. H. Cooley redefined self-concept as being based on how we think others perceive us, including how we think we appear to others and how we think they judge us.

Mark Snyder of the University of Minnesota identified a behavior he called "self-monitoring". In 1972 he developed a test to determine one's level of self-monitoring, which he calls the Self-Monitoring Scale. His definition didn't measure healthy self-awareness, but rather self-adaptation in response to environment and other people. He observed that those who rated highly as self-monitors were pragmatic and adaptable in social situations but struggled in close relationships. He used the word "chameleon-like". We tend to distrust people like this, because they seem to change according to the situation, not revealing their authentic self.

On the other hand, those who rated low on self-monitoring often refuse to be in situations that require them to be inauthentic. Dr. Daniel Goleman, best-known for his work on emotional intelligence, found that extremes in either case, whether refusal to try to fit in at all, or excessive chameleon-like adaptability, can have a negative impact in both the social realm and intimate relationships. When someone refuses to fit in at all, I call this the super-maverick. He or she doesn't make efforts to adapt anywhere! But this tendency leads to other problems, as you can imagine, social and otherwise. We do live in a society that requires a degree of adaptation, but if we're not careful, we'll forget to balance that with our essential selves.

There's a strong distinction between adapting to others' expectations for the purpose of self-protection and the apostle Paul's exhortation for us to be all things to all people in order to win others to Christ. The latter implies a relational *sensitivity* so that we break down barriers for the gospel. This should always be our mode of behavior with nonbelievers. We want to be a fragrance of Christ, yet not sacrifice our unique personality.

To what degree does your self-concept depend on what others think of you, or what you *think* they think? Are you someone who self-monitors when you are in social situations or at work? As the referenced authors and researchers have suggested, and as we all know from experience, a certain amount of social accommodation is needed in life. This helps us function appropriately in our social and work relationships, but *it shouldn't define us or replace our essential self*. If we end up "playing to the crowd" too much, we may feel detached from ourselves. Even if we succeed socially because of the various faces we might project outward, we may unknowingly split from our hearts. Usually, we are unaware of this significant loss in our lives.

Your core self, the real you, is the way God made you. Working in harmony with your true self will best fulfill His will and direction for your life.

Benefits of Knowing Yourself

The benefits of knowing yourself are huge. First, you make YOUR choices, not those of someone else. This leads to more fulfillment, a life "on target". Have you or someone you know ever chosen a friend or career (or even a spouse) based on what someone else wanted, or what you thought you wanted based on someone else's pressure? You can lose years like this, or even your whole life, while missing out on the joy of making your own choices.

Knowing yourself helps you make the best decisions for your life. It saves you much of the second-guessing and worry about the consequences of decisions. It means being connected to your values and living according to them, which many psychologists say is essential for happiness.

Steps for the Journey

To what degree do you feel you know yourself?

Have you ever made decisions in your life which are based on others' expectations instead of what you really wanted? If so, which ones? How could you have decided differently? What difference would that have made for you?

What are the benefits of knowing yourself and who God made you to be?

Record any other reflections before going on to Day Twenty-Seven.

Day Twenty-Seven

Have You Lost Your Way?

Many people don't have enough self-knowledge and the consequences of this can be serious. They can end up in the wrong job, with the wrong spouse, or in the wrong life. They may realize this toward the end of their career or life, or they may never realize it at all. They are overly influenced by what others think, to the point of making choices that aren't right for *them*. They spend their lives being a stranger to themselves. They lose themselves. How tragic.

People who don't know themselves might be confused about what they really want. They can't easily make even small decisions, such as what to wear, how to spend their Saturday afternoon, or bigger ones (Should I get a new job? Is this relationship right for me?) They may firmly believe that they *do* know themselves, having been too deeply ingrained about what they *should* want, to know otherwise.

What are some signs that you may be a stranger to yourself? Maybe you feel "off center" in your work or in your relationships. You may have trouble identifying times of joy in your life, or anything at all which makes you feel delight. How do we lose our way as we grow up? This process starts early on, as family, the church community, and society influence us, either gently or not, to conform to ways of living they consider the best. Much of this training is helpful and even essential to living responsible, mature lives, as well as guiding us in our Christian walk. Yet somewhere along the way, we could begin to ignore the truth inside us about what *we* want and need. You may have been encouraged in your family or your church, for example, to always put others first and never think about what you want. This leads you to pleasing others but losing touch with yourself. Finding the balance is difficult.

While it's good to be considerate and help others, a lifetime of ignoring *your* desires will divorce you from your heart. You can care about others without sacrificing your whole self. It's okay to take care of yourself occasionally, especially when you have to make choices that determine *your* future. The more you know yourself, the more you'll make good decisions. And when you have met your needs and some of your wants, you have more to give to others anyway.

Steps for the Journey

Do you ever feel "off-center" in any area of your life?

How often? In what areas?

Do you think this reflects a temporary situation that fits in with your desires, or misalignment with your "essential self"?

How did you get to this place? Trace any decisions or steps you made, even unconsciously at the time, to get where you are now.

If you don't believe you have major misalignments, what might be smaller areas where you haven't listened to your heart but should have?

What can you do to get back on the right track, or headed in the right direction?

In the next chapter, we'll dig more into this topic and find ways in which you can better connect with your essential self.

Day Twenty-Eight

Glad to Meet Me

One key to knowing what your true self wants is the strong emotion toward or against something that may burst out inside you as you are faced with an option or situation. Martha Beck points out it's when the essential self loudly shouts "yes" or "no". Listen to these responses within yourself. If any emotion is especially strong, either positive or negative, that's a signpost of something your deep essential nature either wants or doesn't want. Of course, you'll also need to evaluate each situation cognitively and Biblically, but don't ignore what your gut has clearly said.

When we know what we think and feel, we make better choices for ourselves, and this empowers us. We give our "power" away to others if we let them influence us too much about our decisions. Our "power" is just a way of saying our volition and responsibility. As I mentioned in a previous section, this is a gift from God. We work with Him by doing our part and trusting Him for His. If you let someone else tell you what to do, control your life, or *make* you angry, you've given away your personal power. If you fashion your life according to others' expectations and desires, you've given away your power. It's like giving part ownership of your life to someone else.

Of course, this doesn't mean always putting yourself first. Listening to your heart in big decisions and life directions won't rule out putting others first in smaller situations as an expression of love or compassion.

Knowing yourself also doesn't rule out asking others for advice or godly counsel. It doesn't mean you don't pray for strength and guidance and rely on God to lead you, as He promised to do. He will use your decisions, the wisdom of others, the wisdom He placed into you, and the transforming power of His Word to guide you. With all this help, you can trust your heart. What your heart says is usually reliable for you, as long as it doesn't contradict God's revealed will. Remember, you are the manager (or steward) of your life, and that's a God-given right and responsibility. Don't give it away to anyone else. Your job is to represent . . . you!

In recent years attention has been given to *self-awareness*, in order to help people overcome interpersonal problems and excel in their careers. These are valid reasons to become more self-aware. However, a far more compelling reason to be self-aware is for *your* sake. Self-awareness leads you to a deeper knowledge of yourself and to a state of being "anchored" or "centered." This gives you a steadier guide to navigate your life. It is difficult to grow spiritually or emotionally without self-awareness. On top of that, a lack of self-awareness can be disastrous in relationships.

Books are available to help you understand your unique personality type, such as *Please Understand Me*, and *Type Talk*, both based on the work of Carl Jung and further developed by other researchers. From this comes the Myers-Briggs Type Indicator, a test that helps determine the general characteristics of your personality. Other tests and theories exist and while they are useful and fascinating tools to help you to understand yourself and others, don't forget to simply listen to your heart. Ask yourself often, what do I think of this? What do I want right now?

Maybe you aren't trying to please another person. The problem might be that you simply don't know yourself very well, having followed the "wise plan for life" that seemed so obvious as you moved along through the years. Now, maybe you aren't so sure it's a fit. You owe it to yourself to take the time to question it and think of possible alternatives. Write these alternatives down and notice your emotional response to each one. Don't be afraid of this process. Reflect on potential misalignments and possible alternatives long before making any changes. That's the place to start.

Impact on Relationships

This important habit plays out in relationships too. How often do you say what you really want to say to another person? How often to you express your real opinion? This doesn't have to always imply something negative or hurtful to someone else, even though some situations require gentle confrontation and clarity.

Sometimes the phrase "say what you feel" is seen as synonymous with being rude and insensitive. It doesn't have to be. In fact, it shouldn't be. If you gently (without strong emotions driving your words) express your honest thoughts, feelings, and opinions, and you've chosen good timing to do so, this can open communication with another person, as well as express your true desire. This kind of authenticity is rare in our day. It reflects a comfort with self and a trust in God for the big picture of our lives.

There are times, however, when being authentic will still evoke hostility. Maybe the other person has gotten comfortable with your false self and doesn't want you to get real, or maybe he or she feels threatened for some other reason. In that case it's often the other person's problem, not yours. With certain people, you may sadly conclude that they won't ever receive your true self. But it's worth it for those who do. Don't stop being honest.

The book *Self Matters*, by Dr. Phil McGraw, is a helpful resource for finding your true self. In it, McGraw writes about the tragedy of people who devote their life energy to denying who they are, thereby wasting their uniqueness. There's treasure in who you are. Don't hide it!

Get to know yourself, the real, core you deep down. Cast off the false selves you identify along the way. Become your own best friend. Learn to be yourself with others, without the need to prove anything. Believe it or not, you will enjoy getting to know yourself, if only you'll give yourself permission. It isn't selfish. It's your obligation, to know the person whose life you're in charge of living. And it's a truly wonderful discovery.

Then let yourself be loved by yourself. Loved by God. Loved by other people. They *will* like the real you once they know you. And you'll feel the same.

Your *real* self is the best version of you.

Steps for the Journey

Take time alone with your journal and ponder the following questions. If you aren't sure what to answer, just give it time and persistence. You'll get to know yourself better.

List your top ten values. Answer truthfully for yourself, not what you think your values ought to be. Then narrow these to five. (For example, things like: family, friendships, contribution, recognition, accomplishment, your faith, variety, aesthetics, challenge, security). Then go back and number these in order of priority. Note any surprises or observations.

1.
2.
3.
4.
5.
6.
7.
8.
9.
10.

My top five values in order:

How large a part do these values play in your daily life and choices? (Hint: If they play a small part, this is a signpost to consider. Maybe your life doesn't correspond to your real self and values.)

What do need in life in order to be happy? Your list can be the first things that come to mind, as well as some of your identified values.

How well are you doing at including these in your life?

These questions will give clues about your current life, indicating if you're on course or not. Do you need adjustments? Have others determined your path for you? What have you learned so far?

How can you know yourself better? Ask yourself the following:

- What do I like?

- What do I dislike?

- Where/when am I happiest?

- Where/when am I most aggravated or unhappy?

- With what kinds of people am I happiest or most aggravated/unhappy?

If someone asks you what you are feeling, would you be able to answer? Ask yourself this question at least 3 times throughout the day. Record your answers in your journal.

Another question to ask is "What do I want *now*?" or "What do I feel like doing right now?" even if you can't go and do it then, you'll learn about your authentic self when you take time to consider your answers.

How comfortable or happy are you spending time in your own company? If you have time by yourself, do you enjoy that, or do you go nearly crazy with boredom and loneliness?

Are there certain areas where your authentic self has recently shouted "YES" or "NO" to something? When you wanted to shout, "I *love* this!" or "Will this *ever* stop?" What were those things? What were you doing when you suddenly felt completely alive or happy? List at least three things for YES and three for NO.

My YES:

My NO:

Would you say that things are falling apart or at least not very good in your life right now?

How might your present circumstances and difficulties be *tools* to help you to find your real self?

How often do you say what you really want to say to another person? For example, "I prefer eating salad tonight", or "I don't want to do that", instead of letting the other person decide or saying, "I don't care"? In more important matters of life, do you express your desires or opinion? What are your patterns?

Are you involved in any ministry activities that are not a fit for you? What keeps you from stopping that activity or looking for something more suited to your preferences and your gifts? Are you worried about letting people down?

Are you really giving people your best self if the activity is not a good fit? How might you plan to change this activity?

How often do you "listen to your gut"? Do you trust what it says? Why or why not? Is it just a habit you haven't developed, to listen to yourself as a reliable guide? Do you sometimes distrust what your heart tells you? If so, why?

Identify factors that stand in your way of living according to your heart. What can you do to remove those obstacles (immediately or over time, depending on what they are)?

What do you believe God thinks about what your heart is telling you? Does He probably agree or disagree? What is the reason for your answer?

Practice right now saying the words, "I don't want to do that," and "I don't want that," or "I prefer this . . ." Write them out and say them out loud, using some typical examples from your life.

Of course, if you're someone who usually pushes for or demands your way (be honest, or ask your significant other or best friend), how can you do the opposite? What can you do to compromise once in a while?

Try stating your opinion or position to someone. Start with a minor situation. (For example, "I can't get together tonight because I'm really tired and want to rest", instead of giving an excuse about how busy you are.) Record your feelings and the results.

Stop and reflect on the fact that God knows you thoroughly at a soul-deep level. He loves and accepts you beyond your understanding. He sees it all, the good and the "needs-improvement". How does that make you feel?

What is this process of exploring this habit teaching you about yourself?

What will you do differently?

"O Lord, you have examined my heart and know everything about me. You know when I sit down or stand up. You know my thoughts even when I'm far away. You see me when I travel and when I rest at home. You know everything I do. You know what I am going to say even before I say it, Lord. You go before me and follow me. You place your hand of blessing on my head. Such knowledge is too wonderful for me, too great for me to understand!" Psalm 139:1-6

Key Thought: God and your heart together know what's best for your life.

Putting it all Together

You've finished learning about the Mental Habits for Believers, but the journey to incorporating them into your life has only just started. Learning and reading is only one step, but predictably, any habit, including mental habits, will take time to adopt.

As you have read through the chapters, it might have seemed like too many separate areas to work on all at once. You might have felt overwhelmed as you considered the changes you want to make in your thinking habits, those that have always been automatic for you. Or it may still feel awkward to question the way you think and try to change your mental talk to yourself. That's normal and okay!

Your mental habits weren't form over a weekend. They won't be restructured by reading once through this or any other book. To begin building these new habits, you'll need to stop, identify, and evaluate your patterns, then *decide* on a different response. Making that crucial decision over and over again will change the habit.

Start working on just *one habit first*. You'll see some satisfying changes and that'll encourage you to keep going. Then you can attack the second habit. They'll seem like separate tasks for a while. However, as you become more comfortable with new habits of thinking, all of them will eventually blend and become second nature for you. You won't be conscious of having eight different habits running in your mind. Together they'll form a new mindset and a way of approaching your life. You'll see the results in a global way, in your emotions, in your relationships, your decisions, in many areas. They will become natural, like breathing. Don't be frustrated by setbacks. They *will* occur. You are trying to change the flow of a long-term thought pattern. Give it time. And keep going. You'll be glad you did.

You'll likely want to reread parts or the whole book. Read it annually or periodically. There may be some that you know you need urgent help with. Start with those. Consider this book a handbook for your future mental development. And don't forget, God will accompany you every step of the way.

If you've done the *Steps for the Journey* exercises and taken time to reflect on each habit, you've likely seen positive shifts in your responses and emotions, and maybe even in your circumstances. Take some time now to reflect on the eight mental habits that you've been studying and make a strategy of continued growth. Some areas will be bigger challenges than others, but all of them can be improved.

You may have already begun to experience an interesting phenomenon: As you read Scripture, you begin seeing everywhere God's exhortations that can only be accomplished in your *mind*. Mental decisions lead to increased faith. Nowhere in Scripture are you told to change your emotions, but repeatedly, you're urged to change your thoughts (which influence your emotions).

Here's an example from the book of Colossians. Paul has just painted a glorious picture of the blessings Christians receive when they come to faith . . . we are brought into His presence, considered holy and blameless, and are reconciled to Him through His Son (Colossians 1:21-22). Then right away in verse 23, we're told the following: "But you must continue to believe this truth and stand firmly in it. Don't drift away from the assurance you received when you heard the Good News." That doesn't mean we'll lose the benefits Paul just described. It *does* mean that we'll lose the *experience* of them if we don't keep standing on those truths. We continue to believe by making a mental decision of belief and appropriation.

Take some time now to evaluate the impact (so far) of the book in your understanding, knowing that with time and practice, the principles will become more anchored, more automatic, and more enriching in your life.

Consider the following habits and note your honest responses.

Your Essential Habit:

Evaluate the habit of placing yourself under God's loving authority each day and trusting Him throughout the day. What changes do you still want and need to make in this area? How is your practice of trusting Him and His character, His ability and promise to guide you, surround, and protect you, provide for your future? This is the foundation for all the habits. Start here and commit yourself to drawing near to Him and trusting Him with everything in your life.

Habit One: Positive Thinking

- Here's how I'm doing

- Here's what I need to improve

- Here's my plan

Habit Two: Interpretations and Mind Frames

- Here's how I'm doing

- Here's what I need to improve

- Here's my plan

Habit Three: Self-Esteem

- Here's how I'm doing

- Here's what I need to improve

- Here's my plan

Habit Four: Living in the Present

- Here's how I'm doing

- Here's what I need to improve

- Here's my plan

Habit Five: Specific Thinking

- Here's how I'm doing

- Here's what I need to improve

- Here's my plan

Habit Six: Self-Responsibility

- Here's how I'm doing

- Here's what I need to improve

- Here's my plan

Habit Seven: Openness

- Here's how I'm doing

- Here's what I need to improve

- Here's my plan

Habit Eight: Knowing Yourself

- Here's how I'm doing

- Here's what I need to improve

- Here's my plan

Other observations, notes, and plans:

You've been challenged toward other ways of thinking, new habits that will change your outlook, alter your emotions, and possibly redirect your future. I hope you have willingly plunged into the chapters and questions, having decided it was worthwhile to invest time and reflection in changing your mental habits.

You may enjoy getting together with a few friends for discussion and accountability, so you'll learn the habits together. This can add fun teamwork to the experience of changing your thinking. You'll find **questions for group discussion** in the next section of the book.

It'll take concentration and persistence and even a bit of failure at times to see new habits spring to life and become rooted in your daily experience. Don't give up. Repetition and practice are the keys to acquiring any new habit.

If you find yourself at an impasse, in your emotions or in a situation, here's an idea: take out a piece of paper and write down three things you can *do* about whatever is making you frustrated or unhappy. It will orient your mind to what *you* can do. This will automatically reinforce the Mental Habit of Self-Responsibility, and this will help unblock the others as well.

Changing some of your mental habits will bring more peace and forward movement into your life, leading you to a happier more fulfilled life aligned with God's desires for you. That's a worthwhile goal that affects your whole future! God is your guide and your compass in this worthy adventure of changing your mental habits, the rudder of your whole life experience.

Thank you for purchasing the *Mental Habits for Believers: 28 Days to New Thought Patterns*. I hope it has met your expectations and begun to transform your mental habits and life!

If you enjoyed the book and found it helpful, please consider leaving a review on the storefront where you purchased it so that others can discover how to improve their mental habits! Thank you!

And . . . if you like inspirational, uplifting **fiction**, visit my website for a complete list of my novels.

Kyle Hunter

www.Kyle-Hunter.com

Questions for Group Discussion

Let's face it, it's difficult to develop new, healthy habits. How much easier, though, if you gather some friends who have the same desires to grow and improve their mental habits. Go through the book together and keep each other accountable. You can share experiences, struggles, and help each other with solutions. You'll have a team of fellow-travelers on the journey, and this will help you all get there faster.

The Mental Habits have been helpful for me personally. When I first did them in a group, we were all amazed and encouraged at the collective insights and shared experiences of each person in the group. It was a rich and rewarding experience, drew us closer as friends, and helped us to do the work together.

With this in mind, I have included some discussion questions in the following pages of the book. Feel free to use these questions as springboards for your discussion.

Some suggestions for group study of the Mental Habits

- There are probably a lot more questions than you'll have time for in one session. If you are the facilitator of the group (or if you are taking turns facilitating), first read the chapter thoroughly, including the questions. If you have less time, mark the questions you want to cover first and break the session in half. If you find you have time, you can go back to the other questions. If you prefer, though, take the questions in order and get as far as you can in the time you have.

- Each group member should have a copy of *Mental Habits for Believers*. Start the session by asking group members how practicing the habit went for them during that week. Spend the first few minutes sharing before going to the topic for that week.

- Some questions are ideal for brainstorming. Here's how that works. Group members help one member come up with solutions to his or her situation, for example, developing a new interpretation for a situation or dealing with worry. Then the whole group can benefit as each of the others in the group take turns sharing their challenges. This will unite the group in thinking of solutions, which will not only help the person, but will reinforce their processing of the new positive habit. Group members can pray for one another at the end of the session and during the week.

- You can do one or two sessions per habit. Depending on the group's needs, gauge how long to spend on each habit. At least one session per habit is the best minimum. Topics such as self-esteem and knowing yourself might require more time.

- Above all, don't be afraid to be open and share with the group (with a commitment to confidentiality) and help one another strengthen their mental habits. It will help you all individually and bring you closer as you help each other and share your lives together.

Do I Have Mental Habits?

- Would you agree that habits involve thoughts (mental) as well as actions? What are some examples in your life?

- What are some of your good habits? Some negative ones? What makes them positive or negative?

- Do you think the Bible addresses mental habits? What are some biblical principles that might apply? Look at Philippians 4:8, Romans 12:3, and Philippians 4:6.

- How would you define "sound judgment"? Is this only spiritual?

- Psalm 104:34 "Let my meditation be pleasing to Him; As for me, I shall be glad in the Lord." (NASB version) What do you think this means? How does it look? Is it only spiritual?

- In your opinion, does reading God's Word regularly automatically give us good habits? What are some examples of what reading the Word regularly *can* do for you in comparison to what it probably will *not* do for you? What is your role? Have you had any experiences that would illustrate this?

- How do you respond to the idea that we have a responsibility for our happiness? Agree, disagree? How and why?

- How can our thoughts affect our happiness or sense of well-being? Can you think of any examples?

- How do our thoughts affect our ability to claim God's promises?

- The text claims that sometimes it is more difficult to change a mental habit than a lifestyle habit. Do you agree? Why or why not? Some examples?

The Habit of Positive Thinking

- What comes to your mind when you think of the phrase "positive thinking"?

- Do Christians also have trouble thinking positively? Why might that be?

- Do you agree that negative thinking is an epidemic? What effect does this have on the society, and on you personally? Examples?

- Do you think God wants us to think positively? Why or why not?

- Do you think this happens in the church? How often is positive thinking only an outward appearance of faith?

- Philippians 4:4 says, "Rejoice in the Lord always". How do you define this, and what are the limitations? How can we add to this?

- What might be a good balance between realistic thinking and positive thinking?

- What kind of things might underlie a habit of negative thinking and talking?

- Refer to the example of Laura on Day 5. Do you think her solution would work? Have you ever tried something like this? Are you willing to try it?

- STOP now and write out one thing that is not so good in your life. Share it. Now reframe it into something positive. Share it.

- STOP now and share 3 things (write 10 at home) that are going right in your life. Share them.

- Do you tend to think negatively? What kinds of situations trigger this? Discuss this in your group. This week make observations on how often you do this and what is behind it. Then try to reframe those things.

- Are there any factors that influence you toward negative thinking? What are they? Is it possible to avoid or minimize these influences? What can you do?

- In the coming week: 1) Apply the steps in days 4, 5, and 6 if you haven't already. 2) Notice any victories you have by applying these principles.

Interpretations and Mind Frames

- What is your response to the statement that how you interpret a situation influences your emotions? Could it change the course of our lives?

- Do any examples from your life or someone else's come to mind?

- What is your response to Dr. McGraw's assertion that there is no reality, only perception? (Dr. Phil McGraw, Day 6) To what extent might this be true?

- Where do filters come from? (Day 7)

- What are some filters you might have that influence the way you interpret situations? (A filter can also be an assumption.)

- Are these filters helpful or simply wrong? Are you willing to challenge them? How would you do this?

- Consider the statement: "Events are most often just random and neutral, but you may interpret as either good or bad." (Day 8) Do you agree? Disagree?

- Do you have assumptions about life that guide your interpretations? What are they? Are they helpful? Do you need to change them?

- Think of one situation, how you interpreted it, and then another possible explanation (interpretation) of what happened. Each group member share one. If the person sharing has difficulty coming up with an alternate interpretation, other group members can make suggestions.

- What interpretation (s) do you most identify with? 1) Life is a daily struggle, 2) It's up to me to make things work, 3) Generally, life is pretty good. Can you add others?

- Are there any specific situations in your past where your "filter" was a negative interpretation? What was the result? How would you change the interpretation? How would that have changed the result?

- What are some ways you could challenge negative interpretations (or filters)?

- What about asking the question, "Are you sure? How do you know?"

- How could being a believer affect the way we interpret events in our lives? What are some interpretations or assumptions we get from Scripture? (Romans 8:28)

- Members of the group can share other verses that could help us in our daily interpretations.

- How did you react to the list of "shoulds"? (Day 8) Do you have any "shoulds"? (If not, you'll probably identify a few as you go through the questions in the coming week!)

- As Christians, what is an alternate way we could look at a negative interpretation or a "should"?

- Think of a negative situation in your life (for example, a job situation, loneliness). Explain how you have been interpreting it. Now find another interpretation you can give to the same situation. How have you grown, or how could you grow spiritually and/or emotionally from this situation?

- Do you ever make negative comparisons of yourself? Why do you do that? How can you change that interpretation? The group members can make suggestions and help each other.

MIND FRAMES
- What was your response to the section on mind frames? Can you identify with the process described? Have you ever tried anything like this? Did it work? Why or why not?

- How would you summarize "changing your frame?"

- Do you have any situations in your life that arise occasionally for which you could benefit from changing your frame? What are they? How does this affect you emotionally? How can you change your frame?

- As a group, help the person who shared find another frame or interpretations for the situation. Anyone who wants to takes a turn. Use principles of positive thinking if that helps.

- As a group, brainstorm some ways to "change the frame."

- Do the exercises this week. Come back with observations about

  What interpretations you have in certain situations.

  How they made you feel.

  Any efforts you made to change them.

  Results of these efforts.

  What you felt God taught you through the exercise.

The Self-Esteem Habit

- What are your initial thoughts about the area of self-esteem? Is it important? Why or why not?

- Did any of your impressions change after reading this chapter? Do you agree or disagree with the summary from Nathaniel Branden? (Day 10)

- How do you think becoming a believer in Christ can affect a person's self-esteem? Is this enough by itself to change our view of ourselves? Why or why not?

- Is high self-esteem the same thing as pride or arrogance? If not, what are the differences?

- What are some signs of low self-esteem? Average self-esteem? High/healthy self-esteem?

- Do you identify yourself in one of these 3 categories? Do you have thoughts or ideas about why that is the case?

- What kinds of factors make the difference?

- Do you agree with the idea that we all have value and talents before we come to Christ (and after) because God created us? How does that make you feel?

- Do you feel like it is selfish to focus on your self-esteem in order to improve it? If so, would it also be selfish to improve other areas of your life, such as your health or education? Does this seem inconsistent to you?

- How could having a higher self-esteem make you happier and more effective in your life?

- What would be some advantages for you? How do you think God would feel about those changes?

- Would you like to share any reasons your self-esteem might be lower than it should be?

- What role do your thoughts play in your self-esteem?

- Do you think your self-esteem can be changed? According to the chapter, what are some tools that might help?

- Did you receive any negative messages (verbal or nonverbal) when you were young from parents or friends? How can you rewrite those messages?

- What are some negative things you say about yourself? As a group, help each other to rewrite the negative statements into positive, affirming ones.

- What are some areas where you have the hardest time in your self-esteem? Or are there certain moments, or certain situations that make you feel worse about yourself?

- What can you learn about those areas mentioned above? What does it tell you about your feelings about yourself?

- What do you think of affirmations? Have you ever tried affirmations? Are you willing to try some?

  Each member can create and say aloud an affirmation to try it. Then they will use that affirmation during the week.

- Do you feel you understand the importance of personal as opposed to Biblical affirmations? How can these personal affirmations affect you in a different way than Biblical affirmations?

- Why might you want to start with personal affirmations before using spiritual or Biblical affirmations? How can you see the two working together?

- What are some ways you can see yourself the way God sees you?

- What do you think of the concept that *you can begin to think of yourself as you want to be rather than as you are* (and with time this will boost your real feelings about who you are)?

The Habit of Living in the Present

- How would you define living in the present?

- What are some ways we DON'T live in the present? Where would you say you live the most often? Future? Present? Past?

- What do you think it means to live consciously?

- Read Colossians 4:5. How does this passage fit into the idea of living in the present?

- How did you respond to the idea that only in the present do we have the power to act? How can this thought impact the future?

- If you struggle with regrets or bitterness over events in the past, what are some ways you can let it go? (In the group, feel free to discuss this with each one who responds, if he or she desires.)

- How inclined are you to worry about the future? Does your faith in God help you with this (really)? If not, why do you think it doesn't? What are some things that may help?

- Are you a planner? Why or why not? Does planning sometimes get out of hand? How could you keep it in perspective?

- What do you think of this statement by Thomas Carlyle, "Our main business is not to see what lies dimly at a distance, but to do what lies clearly at hand."? (Day 16)

- Read and consider the following verses:

"Give all your worries and cares to God, for he cares about you." 1 Peter 5:7.

"Don't worry about anything; instead, pray about everything. Tell God what you need and thank him for all he has done." Philippians 4:6.

- Discuss the impact of these scriptures. Do you believe them, or have trouble believing? Why?

"The Lord says, 'I will guide you along the best pathway for your life. I will advise you and watch over you.'" Psalm 32:8. How will you apply this to your practice of living in the present?

- How will you strengthen your view of God's care over your life?

- Do you have anything you need to let go of? (Worries, regrets, bitterness, anxiety over unknowns, persistent questions.) Take time now to pray for each other, and/or commit to praying this week for one other person in the group.

The Habit of Specific Thinking

- How would you describe "specific thinking" in your own words?

- What is one example of global thinking and one of specific thinking. Share these with the group.

- Can you identify any situations in your life where you have practiced global thinking? How could you take it apart to see the specific sections? How might that change your view?

- Recall a time when information was passed along among people you know. How did you react?

- What does it mean to "own your thoughts and opinions?"

- Would you say that you are a critical thinker? Or are you more likely to accept something without thinking, if it comes from a source you don't question?

- How can you improve in critical, specific thinking?

- Do you have any knee-jerk reactions? If so, in what areas? How can you question your conviction and see it differently?

- Do you agree that some Christians fall into "group thinking" instead of examining an issue for themselves? What are some examples?

- How might specific thinking make us more patient and more loving to others?

The Habit of Self-Responsibility

- What are some ways in which you think God calls on us to use our will?

- What are some disadvantages of being passive?

- Do you agree that you are responsible for your choices and much of what happens to you? How do your actions interweave with God's direction in your life?

- Recall the example of Joe from Day 19. Do you know anyone like him? What is the situation? What could that person do to be more proactive? (Don't mention real names.)

- Do you have any situations similar to Joe's, where you have been passive up to now? What are some steps to take? Group members can brainstorm for suggestions.

- What do you think of the phrase from Day 19, *"our desire or lack of desire is often an inner signal that the Holy Spirit uses to guide us."* Do you agree or disagree? How has this worked in your life in the past?

- Is there anything in your life that you don't or didn't like that you later realized was your fault or your own doing? What is an example?

- Consider a situation you've had for at least six months. Imagine having this same problem five years from now. How does that make you feel? What can you do NOW to change that outcome?

- Is there any area where you've been taking responsibility where you should *not* be, for example, in someone else's life?

- Is there anything holding you back from taking responsibility for something in your life? (Fear of failure, self-doubt or inferiority feelings, fear of success?)

What is one step you can take this week and share with the group next time? Ask the group to pray for your efforts during this week.

The Habit of Openness

- Do you personally know anyone who fits the description in Day 23? What is your impression of that person? What do you like about him or her?

- Do you consider yourself to be a person who is more open, or more closed?

- What would it take for you to become more open?

- How can being more open help us in relationships?

- Do you feel like being open would compromise your faith? Why? Are there ways you can protect your convictions and still enlarge your perspective? Brainstorm about this in the group.

- Do you know people (or are you one) who tends to accept nearly anything coming from a Christian friend or a source that claims to be Christian?

- What does critical thinking mean for you?

- How does being open reflect Christlikeness?

- Jesus spent time with people very different from Himself, with different lifestyles and values. How do you think those people felt with Him?

- Consider your life for a moment. Would you say you have stopped learning and growing?

- What was a difficult situation in your life that made you more open, more patient, or more understanding?

- If the whole world is a buffet table, what are some things you'd like to sample?

- Do you feel that you are willing to grow and change? What is the evidence for your answer?

- Did anything else in the chapter strike you as something you'd like to work on? (For example, having more relationships with people from different cultures or lifestyles, becoming a better listener, etc.)

- Do you identify with any of these as an area to improve?

The Habit of Knowing Yourself

- Why is this perhaps the most important of all the mental habits?

- How could knowing yourself better make you more content?

- Do you agree that you are the point of reference for your life (among humans)? How does that fit with God's role in your life?

- How do you define the social self and the essential self? Have you seen the difference in the activity of your "social self" and your "essential self?

- Are there any areas of your life where you feel you haven't lived according to your heart? Have you let others influence you, or always followed the "shoulds" of other people or society? What areas?

- What are some ways you can reclaim these areas mentioned above? Feel free to brainstorm together as a group.

- Do you feel guilty if you follow your heart, or take care of yourself? If you say, "no" for something that isn't right for you? Why? Will you take steps to change your decisions?

- List a few things that are shouting "yes" or "no" for you. Are these things you practice in your life? Share them with the group.

- What does God think about your "yeses" and "nos?"

- Discuss whether you might need to make any changes. (in reference to "yeses" and "nos").

- What does it mean to take back your "power" or to be empowered?

- Is there anything in your life that you aren't sure it's a fit? What could you do to begin to change this?

- How willing are you to tell people what you truly think and feel? Is this difficult? In what circumstances? Are you willing to try it?

- Is it scary to get to know the real you? Why or why not?

- Are there any other responses from your Journal that you'd like to discuss together?

Additional Notes:

About the Author

Kyle Hunter has observed firsthand the benefits of developing positive mental habits in her work in counseling, social work, and ministry. She has a master's degree in counseling and lived in France for 13 years. She currently lives in North Carolina where she writes inspirational fiction and nonfiction and teaches French to adults.

Check out her inspirational fiction at www.Kyle-Hunter.com. Sign up for newsletters and get a free novella, *Marissa Rewritten*.

www.ingramcontent.com/pod-product-compliance
Lightning Source LLC
Chambersburg PA
CBHW070423010526
44118CB00014B/1883